Leonardo da Vinci

A PSYCHOSEXUAL STUDY OF AN INFANTILE REMINISCENCE

BY

PROFESSOR DR. SIGMUND FREUD, LL.D.

(UNIVERSITY OF VIENNA)

TRANSLATED BY

A. A. BRILL, PH.B., M.D.

Lecturer in Psychoanalysis and Abnormal
Psychology, New York University

ISBN: 978-1-63182-882-9

Printed: March 2023

Published and Distributed By:
Lushena Books
607 Country Club Drive, Unit E
Bensenville, IL 60106
www.lushenabks.com

ISBN: 978-1-63182-882-9

ILLUSTRATIONS

LEONARDO DA VINCI

I

WHEN psychoanalytic investigation, which
usually contents itself with frail human material, approaches the great personages of humanity, it is not impelled to it by motives which
are often attributed to it by laymen. It does
not strive "to blacken the radiant and to drag
the sublime into the mire"; it finds no satisfaction in diminishing the distance between the
perfection of the great and the inadequacy of
the ordinary objects. But it cannot help find-
ing that everything is worthy of understanding
that can be perceived through those prototypes,
and it also believes that none is so big as to be
ashamed of being subject to the laws which control the normal and morbid actions with the
same strictness.

Leonardo da Vinci (1452–1519) was admired even by his contemporaries as one of the greatest men of the Italian Renaissance, still even then he appeared as mysterious to them as he now appears to us. An all-sided genius, "whose form can only be divined but never deeply fathomed," [1] he exerted the most decisive influence on his time as an artist; and it remained to us to recognize his greatness as a naturalist which was united in him with the artist. Although he left masterpieces of the art of painting, while his scientific discoveries remained unpublished and unused, the investigator in him has never quite left the artist, often it has severely injured the artist and in the end it has perhaps suppressed the artist altogether. According to Vasari, Leonardo reproached himself during the last hour of his life for having insulted God and men because he has not done his duty to his art.[2] And even if Vasari's story lacks all probability and belongs to those legends which began to be woven about the mystic master while he was still liv-

[1] In the words of J. Burckhard, cited by Alexandra Konstantinowa, Die Entwicklung des Madonnentypus by Leonardo da Vinci, Strassburg, 1907.
[2] Vite, etc. LXXXIII. 1550–1584.

ing, it nevertheless retains indisputable value as a testimonial of the judgment of those people and of those times.

What was it that removed the personality of Leonardo from the understanding of his contemporaries? Certainly not the many sidedness of his capacities and knowledge, which allowed him to install himself as a player of the lyre on an instrument invented by himself, in the court of Lodovico Sforza, nicknamed Il Moro, the Duke of Milan, or which allowed him to write to the same person that remarkable letter in which he boasts of his abilities as a civil and military engineer. For the combination of manifold talents in the same person was not unusual in the times of the Renaissance; to be sure Leonardo himself furnished one of the most splendid examples of such persons. Nor did he belong to that type of genial persons who are outwardly poorly endowed by nature, and who on their side place no value on the outer forms of life, and in the painful gloominess of their feelings fly from human relations. On the contrary he was tall and symmetrically built, of consummate beauty of countenance and of unusual physical strength, he was charming in his manner, a master of speech, and jovial and affectionate to everybody. He loved beauty in the objects of his surroundings, he was fond of wearing magnificent garments and appreciated every refinement of conduct. In his treatise [3] on the art of painting he compares in a significant passage the art of painting with its sister arts and thus discusses the difficulties of the sculptor: "Now his face is entirely smeared and powdered with marble dust, so that he looks like a baker, he is covered with small marble splinters, so that it seems as if it snowed on his back, and his house is full of stone splinters, and dust. The case of the painter is quite different from that; for the painter is well dressed and sits with great comfort before his work, he gently and very lightly brushes in the beautiful colors. He wears as decorative clothes as he likes, and his house is filled with beautiful paintings and is spotlessly clean. He often enjoys company, music, or some one may

[3] Traktat von der Malerei, new edition and introduction by Marie Herzfeld, E. Diederichs, Jena, 1909.

read for him various nice works, and all this can be listened to with great pleasure, undisturbed by any pounding from the hammer and other noises."

It is quite possible that the conception of a beaming jovial and happy Leonardo was true only for the first and longer period of the master's life. From now on, when the downfall of the rule of Lodovico Moro forced him to leave Milan, his sphere of action and his assured position, to lead an unsteady and unsuccessful life until his last asylum in France, it is possible that the luster of his disposition became pale and some odd features of his character became more prominent. The turning of his interest from his art to science which increased with age must have also been responsible for widening the gap between himself and his contemporaries. All his efforts with which, according to their opinion, he wasted his time instead of diligently filling orders and becoming rich as perhaps his former classmate Perugino, seemed to his contemporaries as capricious playing, or even caused them to suspect him of being in the service of the "black art." We who know him from his sketches understand him better. In a time in which the authority of the church began to be substituted by that of antiquity and in which only theoretical investigation existed, he the forerunner, or better the worthy competitor of Bacon and Copernicus, was necessarily isolated. When he dissected cadavers of horses and human beings, and built flying apparatus, or when he studied the nourishment of plants and their behavior towards poisons, he naturally deviated much from the commentators of Aristotle and came nearer the despised alchemists, in whose laboratories the experimental investigations found some refuge during these unfavorable times.

The effect that this had on his paintings was that he disliked to handle the brush, he painted less and what was more often the case, the things he began were mostly left unfinished; he cared less and less for the future fate of his works. It was this mode of working that was held up to him as a reproach from his contemporaries to whom his behavior to his art remained a riddle.

Many of Leonardo's later admirers have attempted to wipe off the stain of unsteadiness from his character. They maintained that what is blamed in Leonardo is a general characteristic of great artists. They said that even the energetic Michelangelo who was absorbed in his work left many incompleted works, which was as little due to his fault as to Leonardo's in the same case. Besides some pictures were not as unfinished as he claimed, and what the layman would call a masterpiece may still appear to the creator of the work of art as an unsatisfied embodiment of his intentions; he has a faint notion of a perfection which he despairs of reproducing in likeness. Least of all should the artist be held responsible for the fate which befalls his works.

As plausible as some of these excuses may sound they nevertheless do not explain the whole state of affairs which we find in Leonardo. The painful struggle with the work, the final flight from it and the indifference to its future fate may be seen in many other artists, but this behavior is shown in Leonardo to highest degree. Edm. Solmi [4] cites (p. 12) the expression of one of his pupils: "Pareva, che ad ogni ora tremasse, quando si poneva a dipingere, e però no diede mai fine ad alcuna cosa cominciata, considerando la grandezza dell'arte, tal che egli scorgeva errori in quelle cose, che ad altri parevano miracoli." His last pictures, Leda, the Madonna di Saint Onofrio, Bacchus and St. John the Baptist, remained unfinished "come quasi intervenne di tutte le cose sue." Lomazzo,[5] who finished a copy of The Holy Supper, refers in a sonnet to the familiar inability of Leonardo to finish his works:

"Protogen che il penel di sue pitture
Non levava, agguaglio il Vinci Divo,
Di cui opra non è finita pure."

The slowness with which Leonardo worked was proverbial. After the most thorough preliminary studies he painted The Holy Supper for three years in the cloister of Santa Maria

[4] Solmi. La resurrezione dell' opera di Leonardo in the collected work; Leonardo da Vinci. Conferenze Fiorentine, Milan, 1910.
[5] Scognamiglio Ricerche e Documenti sulla giovinezza di Leonardo da Vinci. Napoli, 1900.

delle Grazie in Milan. One of his contemporaries, Matteo Bandelli, the writer of novels, who was then a young monk in the cloister, relates that Leonardo often ascended the scaffold very early in the morning and did not leave the brush out of his hand until twilight, never thinking of eating or drinking. Then days passed without putting his hand on it, sometimes he remained for hours before the painting and derived satisfaction from studying it by himself. At other times he came directly to the cloister from the palace of the Milanese Castle where he formed the model of the equestrian statue for Francesco Sforza, in order to add a few strokes with the brush to one of the figures and then stopped immediately.[6] According to Vasari he worked for years on the portrait of Monna Lisa, the wife of the Florentine de Gioconda, without being able to bring it to completion. This circumstance may also account for the fact that it was never delivered to the one who ordered it but remained with Leonardo who took it with him to

[6] W. v. Seidlitz. Leonardo da Vinci, der Wendepunkt der Renaissance, 1909, Bd. I, p. 203.

France.[7] Having been procured by King Francis I, it now forms one of the greatest treasures of the Louvre.

When one compares these reports about Leonardo's way of working with the evidence of the extraordinary amount of sketches and studies left by him, one is bound altogether to reject the idea that traits of flightiness and unsteadiness exerted the slightest influence on Leonardo's relation to his art. On the contrary one notices a very extraordinary absorption in work, a richness in possibilities in which a decision could be reached only hestitatingly, claims which could hardly be satisfied, and an inhibition in the execution which could not even be explained by the inevitable backwardness of the artist behind his ideal purpose. The slowness which was striking in Leonardo's works from the very beginning proved to be a symptom of his inhibition, a forerunner of his turning away from painting which manifested itself later.[8] It was this

[7] W. v. Seidlitz, 1. c. Bd. II, p. 48.
[8] W. Pater. The Renaissance, p. 107, The Macmillan Co., 1910. "But it is certain that at one period of his life he had almost ceased to be an artist."

slowness which decided the not undeserving fate of The Holy Supper. Leonardo could not take kindly to the art of fresco painting which demands quick work while the background is still moist, it was for this reason that he chose oil colors, the drying of which permitted him to complete the picture according to his mood and leisure. But these colors separated themselves from the background upon which they were painted and which isolated them from the brick wall; the blemishes of this wall and the vicissitudes to which the room was subjected seemingly contributed to the inevitable deterioration of the picture.[9]

The picture of the cavalry battle of Anghiari, which in competition with Michelangelo he began to paint later on a wall of the Sala de Consiglio in Florence and which he also left in an unfinished state, seemed to have perished through the failure of a similar technical process. It seems here as if a peculiar interest, that of the experimenter, at first reënforced the artistic, only later to damage the art production.

[9] Cf. v. Seidlitz, Bd. I die Geschichte der Restaurations — und Rettungsversuche.

The character of the man Leonardo evinces
still some other unusual traits and apparent
contradictions. Thus a certain inactivity and ·
indifference seemed very evident in him. At a
time when every individual sought to gain the
widest latitude for his activity, which could not
take place without the development of energetic
aggression towards others, he surprised every
one through his quiet peacefulness, his shun-
ning of all competition and controversies. . He
was mild and kind to all, he was said to have
rejected a meat diet because he did not consider it just to rob animals of their lives, and
one of his special pleasures was to buy caged
birds in the market and set them free.[10]   He
condemned war and bloodshed and designated
man not so much as the king of the animal
world, but rather as the worst of the wild
beasts.[11]   But this effeminate delicacy of feeling did not prevent him from accompanying

[10] Müntz. Léonard de Vinci, Paris, 1899, p. 18. (A letter
of a contemporary from India to a Medici alludes to this peculiarity of Leonardo   Given by Richter: The literary Works
of Leonardo da Vinci.)

[11] F. Botazzi. Leonardo biologo e anatomico. Conferenze
Fiorentine, p. 186, 1910.

condemned criminals on their way to execution
in order to study and sketch in his notebook
their features, distorted by fear, nor did it prevent him from inventing the most cruel offen-
sive weapons, and from entering the service of
Cesare Borgia as chief military engineer.
Often he seemed to be indifferent to good and
evil, or he had to be measured with a special
standard. He held a high position in Cesare's
campaign which gained for this most inconsid-
erate and most faithless of foes the possession
of the Romagna. Not a single line of Leonardo's sketches betrays any criticism or sympathy
of the events of those days. The comparison
with Goethe during the French campaign cannot here be altogether rejected.

If a biographical effort really endeavors to
penetrate the understanding of the psychic life
of its hero it must not, as happens in most biog-
raphies through discretion or prudery, pass
over in silence the sexual activity or the sex
peculiarity of the one examined. What we
know about it in Leonardo is very little but full
of significance. In a period where there was
a constant struggle between riotous licentious-

ness and gloomy asceticism, Leonardo presented an example of cool sexual rejection which one would not expect in an artist and a portrayer of feminine beauty. Solmi [12] cites the following sentence from Leonardo showing his frigidity: "The act of procreation and everything that has any relation to it is so disgusting that human beings would soon die out if it were not a traditional custom and if there were no pretty faces and sensuous dispositions." His posthumous works which not only treat of the greatest scientific problems but also comprise the most guileless objects which to us do not seem worthy of so great a mind (an allegorical natural history,. animal fables, witticisms, prophecies),[13] are chaste to a degree— one might say abstinent—that in a work of *belle lettres* would excite wonder even to-day. They evade everything sexual so thoroughly, as if Eros alone who preserves everything living was no worthy material for the scientific

[12] E. Solmi: Leonardo da Vinci. German Translation by Emmi Hirschberg. Berlin, 1908.
[13] Marie Herzfeld: Leonardo da Vinci der Denker, Forscher und Poet. Second edition. Jena, 1906.

impulse of the investigator.[14]   It is known how
frequently great artists found pleasure in giving vent to their phantasies in erotic and even
grossly obscene representations; in contradis-
tinction to this Leonardo left only some ana-
tomical drawings of the woman's internal genitals, the position of the child in the womb, etc.
It is doubtful whether Leonardo ever embraced a woman in love, nor is it known that
he ever entertained an intimate spiritual relation with a woman as in the case of Michelangelo and Vittoria Colonna.   While he still
lived as an apprentice in the house of his master Verrocchio, he with other young men were
accused of forbidden homosexual relations
which ended in his acquittal.   It seems that he
came into this suspicion because he employed
as a model a boy of evil repute.[15]   When he
was a master he surrounded himself with hand-

[14] His collected witticisms—belle - facezie,—which are not
translated, may be an exception.   Cf. Herzfeld, Leonardo da
Vinci, p. 151.

[15] According to Scognamiglio (l. c. p. 49) reference is made
to this episode in an obscure and even variously interpreted
passage of the Codex Atlanticus: "Quando io feci Domened-
dio putto voi mi metteste in prigione, ora s'io lo fo grande,
voi mi farete peggio."

some boys and youths whom he took as pupils. The last of these pupils Francesco Melzi, accompanied him to France, remained with him until his death, and was named by him as his heir. Without sharing the certainty of his modern biographers, who naturally reject the possibility of a sexual relation between himself and his pupils as a baseless insult to this great man, it may be thought by far more probable that the affectionate relationships of Leonardo to the young men did not result in sexual activity. Nor should one attribute to him a high measure of sexual activity.

The peculiarity of this emotional and sexual life viewed in connection with Leonardo's double nature as an artist and investigator can be grasped only in one way. Of the biographers to whom psychological viewpoints are often very foreign, only one, Edm. Solmi, has to my knowledge approached the solution of the riddle. But a writer, Dimitri Sergewitsch Merejkowski, who selected Leonardo as the hero of a great historical novel has based his delineation on such an understanding of this unusual man, and if not in dry words he gave unmistakable utterance in plastic expression in the manner of a poet.[16] Solmi judges Leonardo as follows: "But the unrequited desire to understand everything surrounding him, and with cold reflection to discover the deepest secret of everything that is perfect, has condemned Leonardo's works to remain forever unfinished."[17] In an essay of the Conferenze Fiorentine the utterances of Leonardo are cited, which show his confession of faith and furnish the key to his character.

"Nessuna cosa si può amare nè odiare, se prima no si ha cognition di quella." [18]

That is: One has no right to love or to hate anything if one has not acquired a thorough knowledge of its nature. And the same is repeated by Leonardo in a passage of the Treaties on the Art of Painting where he seems

[16] Merejkowski: The Romance of Leonardo da Vinci, translated by Herbert Trench, G. P. Putnam Sons, New York. It forms the second of the historical Trilogy entitled Christ and Anti-Christ, of which the first volume is Julian Apostata, and the third volume is Peter the Great and Alexei.

[17] Solmi l. c. p. 46.

[18] Filippo Botazzi, l. c. p. 193.

to defend himself against the accusation of irreligiousness:

"But such censurers might better remain si-
lent. For that action is the manner of showing the workmaster so many wonderful things,
and this is the way to love so great a discoverer.
For, verily great love springs from great
knowledge of the beloved object, and if you
little know it you will be able to love it only
little or not at all." [19]

The value of these utterances of Leonardo
cannot be found in that they impart to us an
important psychological fact, for what they
maintain is obviously false, and Leonardo must
have known this as well as we do. It is not
true that people refrain from loving or hat-
ing until they have studied and became familiar with the nature of the object to whom they
wish to give these affects, on the contrary they
love impulsively and are guided by emotional
motives which have nothing to do with cognition and whose affects are weakened, if anything, by thought and reflection. Leonardo

[19] Marie Herzfeld: Leonardo da Vinci, Traktat von der
Malerei, Jena, 1909 (Chap. I, 64).

only could have implied that the love practiced by people is not of the proper and unobjectionable kind, one should so love as to hold back the affect and to subject it to mental elaboration, and only after it has stood the test of the intellect should free play be given to it. And we thereby understand that he wishes to tell us that this was the case with himself and that it would be worth the effort of everybody else to treat love and hatred as he himself does.

And it seems that in his case it was really so. His affects were controlled and subjected to the investigation impulse, he neither loved nor hated, but questioned himself whence does that arise, which he was to love or hate, and what does it signify, and thus he was at first forced to appear indifferent to good and evil, to beauty and ugliness. During this work of investigation love and hatred threw off their designs and uniformly changed into intellectual interest. As a matter of fact Leonardo was not dispassionate, he did not lack the divine spark which is the mediate or immediate motive power—*il primo motore*—of all human activity. He only transmuted his passion into inquisitiveness. He then applied himself to study with that persistence, steadiness, and profundity which comes from passion, and on the height of the psychic work, after the cognition was won, he allowed the long checked affect to break loose and to flow off freely like a branch of a stream, after it has accomplished its work. At the height of his cognition when he could examine a big part of the whole he was seized with a feeling of pathos, and in ecstatic words he praised the grandeur of that part of creation which he studied, or—in religious cloak—the greatness of the creator. Solmi has correctly divined this process of transformation in Leonardo. According to the quotation of such a passage, in which Leonardo celebrated the higher impulse of nature ("O mirabile necessita . . .") he said: "Tale trasfigurazione della scienza della natura in emozione, quasi direi, religiosa, è uno dei tratti caratteristici de manoscritti vinciani, e si trova cento e cento volte espressa. . . ."[20]

[20] "Such transfiguration of science and of nature into emotions, or one might say, religion, is one of the characteristic traits of da Vinci's manuscripts, which one finds expressed hundreds of times." Solmi: La resurrezione, etc., p. 11.

Leonardo was called the Italian Faust on account of his insatiable and indefatigable desire for investigation. But even if we disregard the fact that it is the possible retransformation of the desire for investigation into the joys of life which is presupposed in the Faust tragedy, one might venture to remark that Leonardo's system recalls Spinoza's mode of thinking.

The transformation of psychic motive power into the different forms of activity is perhaps as little convertible without loss, as in the case of physical powers. Leonardo's example teaches how many other things one must follow up in these processes. Not to love before one gains full knowledge of the thing loved presupposes a delay which is harmful. When one finally reaches cognition he neither loves nor hates properly; one remains beyond love and hatred. One has investigated instead of having loved. It is perhaps for this reason that Leonardo's life was so much poorer in love than those of other great men and great artists. The storming passions of the soul-stirring and consuming kind, in which others experience the best part of their lives, seem to have missed him.

There are still other consequences when one follows Leonardo's dictum. Instead of acting and producing one just investigates. He who begins to divine the grandeur of the universe and its needs readily forgets his own insignificant self. When one is struck with admiration and becomes truly humble he easily forgets that he himself is a part of that living force, and that according to the measure of his own personality he has the right to make an effort to change that destined course of the world, the world in which the insignificant is no less wonderful and important than the great.

Solmi thinks that Leonardo's investigations started with his art,[21] he tried to investigate the attributes and laws of light, of color, of shades and of perspective so as to be sure of becoming a master in the imitation of nature and to be able to show the way to others. It

[21] La resurrezione, etc., p. 8: "Leonardo placed the study of nature as a precept to painting . . . later the passion for study became dominating, he no longer wished to acquire science for art, but science for science' sake."

is probable that already at that time he over-estimated the value of this knowledge for the artist. Following the guide-rope of the painter's need, he was then driven further and further to investigate the objects of the art of painting, such as animals and plants, and the proportions of the human body, and to follow the path from their exterior to their interior structure and biological functions, which really also express themselves in their appearance and should be depicted in art. And finally he was pulled along by this overwhelming desire until the connection was torn from the demands of his art, so that he discovered the general laws of mechanics and divined the history of the stratification and fossilization of the Arno-valley, until he could enter in his book with capital letters the cognition: *Il sole non si move* (The sun does not move). His investigations were thus extended over almost all realms of natural science, in every one of which he was a discoverer or at least a prophet or forerunner.[22] However, his curiosity continued to be directed to the outer world, some-

[22] For an enumeration of his scientific attainments see Marie

thing kept him away from the investigation of the psychic life of men; there was little room for psychology in the "Academia Vinciana," for which he drew very artistic and very complicated emblems.

When he later made the effort to return from his investigations to the art from which he started he felt that he was disturbed by the new paths of his interest and by the changed nature of his psychic work. In the picture he was interested above all in a problem, and behind this one he saw emerging numerous other problems just as he was accustomed in the endless and indeterminable investigations of natural history. He was no longer able to limit his demands, to isolate the work of art, and to tear it out from that great connection of which he knew it formed part. After the most exhausting efforts to bring to expression all that was in him, all that was connected with it in his thoughts, he was forced to leave it unfinished, or to declare it incomplete.

The artist had once taken into his service

Herzfeld's interesting introduction (Jena, 1906) to the essays of the Conferenze Fiorentine, 1910, and elsewhere.

the investigator to assist him, now the servant was stronger and suppressed his master.

When we find in the portrait of a person one single impulse very forcibly developed, as curiosity in the case of Leonardo, we look for the explanation in a special constitution, concerning its probable organic determination hardly anything is known. Our psychoanalytic studies of nervous people lead us to look for two other expectations which we would like to find verified in every case. We consider it probable that this very forcible impulse was already active in the earliest childhood of the person, and that its supreme sway was fixed by infantile impressions; and we further assume that originally it drew upon sexual motive powers for its reënforcement so that it later can take the place of a part of the sexual life. Such person would then, e.g., investigate with that passionate devotion which another would give to his love, and he could investigate instead of loving. We would venture the conclusion of a sexual reënforcement not only in the impulse to investigate, but also in most other cases of special intensity of an impulse.

Observation of daily life shows us that most persons have the capacity to direct a very tangible part of their sexual motive powers to their professional or business activities. The sexual impulse is particularly suited to yield such contributions because it is endowed with the capacity of sublimation, i.e., it has the power to exchange its nearest aim for others of higher value which are not sexual. We consider this process as proved, if the history of childhood or the psychic developmental history of a person shows that in childhood this powerful impulse was in the service of the sexual interest. We consider it a further corroboration if this is substantiated by a striking stunting in the sexual life of mature years, as if a part of the sexual activity had now been replaced by the activity of the predominant impulse.

The application of these assumptions to the case of the predominant investigation-impulse seems to be subject to special difficulties, as one is unwilling to admit that this serious impulse exists in children or that children show any noteworthy sexual interest. However, these difficulties are easily obviated. The untiring pleasure in questioning as seen in little children demonstrates their curiosity, which is puzzling to the grown-up, as long as he does not understand that all these questions are only circumlocutions, and that they cannot come to an end because they replace only one question which the child does not put. When the child becomes older and gains more understanding this manifestation of curiosity suddenly disappears. But psychoanalytic investigation gives us a full explanation in that it teaches us that many, perhaps most children, at least the most gifted ones, go through a period beginning with the third year, which may be designated as the period of *infantile sexual investigation*. As far as we know, the curiosity is not awakened spontaneously in children of this age, but is aroused through the impression of an important experience, through the birth of a little brother or sister, or through fear of the same endangered by some outward experience, wherein the child sees a danger to his egotistic interests. The investigation directs itself to the question whence children come, as if the

child were looking for means to guard against
such undesired event.   We were astonished to
find that the child refuses to give credence to the
information imparted to it, e.g., it energetically
rejects the mythological and so ingenious stork-
fable, we were astonished to find that its
psychic independence dates from this act of dis-
belief, that it often feels itself at serious vari-
ance with the grown-ups, and never forgives
them for having been deceived of the truth on
this occasion.   It investigates in its own way,
it divines that the child is in the mother's
womb, and guided by the feelings of its own
sexuality, it formulates for itself theories about
the origin of children from food, about being
born through the bowels, about the rôle of the
father which is difficult to fathom, and even
at that time it has a vague conception of the
sexual act which appears to the child as something hostile, as something violent.   But as its
own sexual constitution is not yet equal to the
task of producing children, his investigation
whence come children must also run aground
and must be left in the lurch as unfinished.
The impression of this failure at the first at-

tempt of intellectual independence seems to be of a persevering and profoundly depressing nature.[23]

If the period of infantile sexual investigation comes to an end through an impetus of energetic sexual repression, the early association with sexual interest may result in three different possibilities for the future fate of the investigation impulse. The investigation either shares the fate of the sexuality, the curiosity henceforth remains inhibited and the free activity of intelligence may become narrowed for life; this is especially made possible by the powerful religious inhibition of thought, which is brought about shortly hereafter through education. This is the type of neurotic inhibition. We know well that the so acquired mental weakness furnishes effective support for the

[23] For a corroboration of this improbable sounding assertion see the "Analysis of the Phobia of a Five-year-old Boy," Jahrbuch für Psychoanalytische und Psychopathologische Forschungen, Bd. I, 1909, and the similar observation in Bd. II, 1910. In an essay concerning "Infantile Theories of Sex" (Sammlungen kleiner Schriften zur Neurosenlehre, p. 167, Second Series, 1909), I wrote: "But this reasoning and doubting serves as a model for all later intellectual work in problems, and the first failure acts as a paralyzer for all times."

outbreak of a neurotic disease. In a second
type the intellectual development is sufficiently
strong to withstand the sexual repression pull-
ing at it. Sometimes after the disappearance
of the infantile sexual investigation, it offers
its support to the old association in order to
elude the sexual repression, and the suppressed
sexual investigation comes back from the unconscious as compulsive reasoning, it is naturally distorted and not free, but forceful
enough to sexualize even thought itself and to
accentuate the intellectual operations with the
pleasure and fear of the actual sexual processes. Here the investigation becomes sexual
activity and often exclusively so, the feeling of
settling the problem and of explaining things
in the mind is put in place of sexual gratification. But the indeterminate character of the
infantile investigation repeats itself also in the
fact that this reasoning never ends, and that
the desired intellectual feeling of the solution
constantly recedes into the distance. By vir-
tue of a special disposition the third, which is
the most rare and most perfect type, escapes
the inhibition of thought and the compulsive

reasoning. Also here sexual repression takes place, it is unable, however, to direct a partial impulse of the sexual pleasure into the unconscious, but the libido withdraws from the fate of the repression by being sublimated from the beginning into curiosity, and by reënforcing the powerful investigation impulse. Here, too, the investigation becomes more or less compulsive and a substitute of the sexual activity, but owing to the absolute difference of the psychic process behind it (sublimation in place of the emergence from the unconscious) the character of the neurosis does not manifest itself, the subjection to the original complexes of the infantile sexual investigation disappears, and the impulse can freely put itself in the service of the intellectual interest. It takes account of the sexual repression which made it so strong in contributing to it sublimated libido, by avoiding all occupation with sexual themes.

In mentioning the concurrence in Leonardo of the powerful investigation impulse with the stunting of his sexual life which was limited to the so-called ideal homosexuality, we feel inclined to consider him as a model example of our third type. The most essential point of his character and the secret of it seems to lie in the fact, that after utilizing the infantile activity of curiosity in the service of sexual interest he was able to sublimate the greater part of his libido into the impulse of investigation. But to be sure the proof of this conception is not easy to produce. To do this we would have to have an insight into the psychic development of his first childhood years, and it seems foolish to hope for such material when the reports concerning his life are so meager and so uncertain; and moreover, when we deal with information which even persons of our own generation withdraw from the attention of the observer.

We know very little concerning Leonardo's youth. He was born in 1452 in the little city of Vinci between Florence and Empoli; he was an illegitimate child which was surely not considered a great popular stain in that time. His father was Ser Piero da Vinci, a notary and descendant of notaries and farmers, who took their name from the place Vinci; his mother, a certain Caterina, probably a peasant girl, who later married another native of Vinci. Nothing else about his mother appears in the life history of Leonardo, only the writer Merejkowski believed to have found some traces of her. The only definite information about Leonardo's childhood is furnished by a legal document from the year 1457, a register of assessment in which Vinci Leonardo is mentioned among the members of the family as a five-year-old illegitimate child of Ser Piero.[24] As the marriage of Ser Piero with Donna Albiera remained childless the little Leonardo could be brought up in his father's house. He did not leave this house until he entered as apprentice —it is not known what year—in the studio of Andrea del Verrocchio. In 1472 Leonardo's name could already be found in the register of the members of the "Compagnia dei Pittori." That is all.

[24] Scognamiglio l. c., p. 15.

II

As far as I know Leonardo only once interspersed in his scientific descriptions a communication from his childhood. In a passage where he speaks about the flight of the vulture, he suddenly interrupts himself in order to follow up a memory from very early years which came to his mind.

"It seems that it had been destined before that I should occupy myself so thoroughly with the vulture, for it comes to my mind as a very early memory, when I was still in the cradle, a vulture came down to me, he opened my mouth with his tail and struck me a few times with his tail against my lips." [1]

We have here an infantile memory and to be sure of the strangest sort. It is strange on account of its content and account of the time of life in which it was fixed. That a person

[1] Cited by Scognamiglio from the Codex Atlanticus, p. 65.

could retain a memory of the nursing period is perhaps not impossible, but it can in no way be taken as certain. But what this memory of Leonardo states, namely, that a vulture opened the child's mouth with its tail, sounds so improbable, so fabulous, that another conception which puts an end to the two difficulties with one stroke appeals much more to our judgment. The scene of the vulture is not a memory of Leonardo, but a phantasy which he formed later, and transferred into his childhood. The childhood memories of persons often have no different origin, as a matter of fact, they are not fixated from an experience like the conscious memories from the time of maturity and then repeated, but they are not produced until a later period when childhood is already past, they are then changed and disguised and put in the service of later tendencies, so that in general they cannot be strictly differentiated from phantasies. Their nature will perhaps be best understood by recalling the manner in which history writing originated among ancient nations. As long as the nation was small and weak it gave no thought to the writing of its history, it tilled the soil of its land, defended its existence against its neighbors by seeking to wrest land from them and endeavored to become rich. It was a heroic but unhistoric time. Then came another age, a period of self-realization in which one felt rich and powerful, and it was then that one experienced the need to discover whence one originated and how one developed. The history-writing which then continues to register the present events throws also its backward glance to the past, it gathers traditions and legends, it interprets what survived from olden times into customs and uses, and thus creates a history of past ages. It is quite natural that this history of the past ages is more the expressions of opinions and desires of the present than a faithful picture of the past, for many a thing escaped the people's memory, other things became distorted, some trace of the past was misunderstood and interpreted in the sense of the present; and besides one does not write history through motives of objective curiosity, but because one desires to impress his contemporaries, to stimulate and extol them, or to hold the mirror before them. The conscious memory of a person concerning the experiences of his maturity may now be fully compared to that of history writing, and his infantile memories, as far as their origin and reliability are concerned will actually correspond to the history of the primitive period of a people which was compiled later with purposive intent.

Now one may think that if Leonardo's story of the vulture which visited him in his cradle is only a phantasy of later birth, it is hardly worth while giving more time to it. One could easily explain it by his openly avowed inclination to occupy himself with the problem of the flight of the bird which would lend to this phantasy an air of predetermined fate. But with this depreciation one commits as great an injustice as if one would simply ignore the material of legends, traditions, and interpretations in the primitive history of a people. Notwithstanding all distortions and misunderstandings to the contrary they still represent the reality of the past; they represent what the people formed out of the experiences of its past age under the domination of once powerful and

to-day still effective motives, and if these distortions could be unraveled through the knowledge of all effective forces, one would surely
discover the historic truth under this legendary
material. The same holds true for the infantile reminiscences or for the phantasies of indi-
viduals. What a person thinks he recalls from
his·childhood, is not of an indifferent nature.
As a rule the memory remnants, which he himself does not understand, conceal invaluable
evidences of the most important features of his
psychic development. As the psychoanalytic
technique affords us excellent means for bringing to light this concealed material, we shall
venture the attempt to fill the gaps in the history of Leonardo's life through the analysis of
his infantile phantasy. And if we should not
attain a satisfactory degree of certainty, we
will have to console ourselves with the fact that
so many other investigations about this great
and mysterious man have met no better fate.

When we examine Leonardo's vulture-phantasy with the eyes of a psychoanalyst then it
does not seem strange very long; we recall that
we have often found similar structures in

dreams, so that we may venture to translate this phantasy from its strange language into words that are universally understood. The translation then follows an erotic direction. Tail, "coda," is one of the most familiar symbols, as well as a substitutive designation of the male member which is no less true in Italian than in other languages. The situation contained in the phantasy, that a vulture opened the mouth of the child and forcefully belabored it with its tail, corresponds to the idea of fellatio, a sexual act in which the member is placed into the mouth of the other person. Strangely enough this phantasy is altogether of a passive character; it resembles certain dreams and phantasies of women and of passive homosexuals who play the feminine part in sexual relations.

Let the reader be patient for a while and not flare up with indignation and refuse to follow psychoanalysis because in its very first applications it leads to an unpardonable slander of the memory of a great and pure man. For it is quite certain that this indignation will never solve for us the meaning of Leonardo's childhood phantasy; on the other hand, Leonardo has unequivocally acknowledged this phantasy, and we shall therefore not relinquish the expectation—or if you prefer the preconception—that like every psychic production such as dreams, visions and deliria this phantasy, too, must have some meaning. Let us therefore lend our unprejudiced ears for a while to psychoanalytic work which after all has not yet uttered the last word.

The desire to take the male member into the mouth and suck it, which is considered as one of the most disgusting of sexual perversions, is nevertheless a frequent occurrence among the women of our time—and as shown in old sculptures was the same in earlier times—and in the state of being in love seems to lose entirely its disgusting character. The physician encounters phantasies based on this desire, even in women who did not come to the knowledge of the possibility of such sexual gratification by reading v. Krafft-Ebing's Psychopathia Sexualis or through other information. It seems that it is quite easy for the women themselves to produce such wish-phantasies.[2]   Investigation then teaches us that this situation, so forcibly condemned by custom, may be traced to the most harmless origin.   It is nothing but the elaboration of another situation in which we all once felt comfort, namely, when we were in the suckling-age ("when I was still in the cradle") and took the nipple of our mother's or wet-nurse's breast into our mouth to suck it.   The organic impression of this first pleasure in our lives surely remains indelibly impregnated; when the child later learns to know the udder of the cow, which in function is a breast-nipple, but in shape and in position on the abdomen resembles the penis, it obtains the primary basis for the later formation of that disgusting sexual phantasy.

We now understand why Leonardo displaced the memory of the supposed experience with the vulture to his nursing period.   This phantasy conceals nothing more or less than a reminiscence of nursing—or being nursed—at the mother's breast, a scene both human and beautiful, which he as well as other artists under-

[2] Cf. here the "Bruchstück einer Hysterieanalyse," in Neurosenlehre, Second series, 1909.

took to depict with the brush in the form of the mother of God and her child.   At all events, we also wish to maintain, something we do not as yet understand, that this reminiscence, equally significant for both sexes, was elaborated in the man Leonardo into a passive homosexual phantasy.   For the present we shall not take up the question as to what connection there is between homosexuality and suckling at the mother's breast, we merely wish to recall that tradition actually designates Leonardo as a person of homosexual feelings.   In considering this, it makes no difference whether that accusation against the youth Leonardo was justified or not.   It is not the real activity but the nature of the feeling which causes us to decide whether to attribute to some one the characteristic of homosexuality.

Another incomprehensible feature of Leonardo's infantile phantasy next claims our interest.   We interpret the phantasy of being wet-nursed by the mother and find that the mother is replaced by a vulture.   Where does this vulture originate and how does he come into this place?

A thought now obtrudes itself which seems so remote that one is tempted to ignore it. In the sacred hieroglyphics of the old Egyptians the mother is represented by the picture of the vulture.[3] These Egyptians also worshiped a motherly deity, whose head was vulture like, or who had many heads of which at least one or two was that of a vulture.[4] The name of this goddess was pronounced *Mut;* we may question whether the sound similarity to our word mother (Mutter) is only accidental? So the vulture really has some connection with the mother, but of what help is that to us? Have we a right to attribute this knowledge to Leonardo when François Champollion first succeeded in reading hieroglyphics between 1790–1832?[5]

It would also be interesting to discover in what way the old Egyptians came to choose the vulture as a symbol of motherhood. As a matter of fact the religion and culture of Egyptians

[3] Horapollo: Hieroglyphica I, 11. Μητέρα δὲ γράφοντες ... γῦπα ζωγραφοῦσιν.

[4] Roscher: Ausf. Lexicon der griechischen und römischen Mythologie. Artikel Mut, II Bd., 1894-1897.—Lanzone. Dizionario di Mitologia egizia. Torino, 1882.

[5] H. Hartleben, Champollion. Sein Leben und sein Werk, 1906.

were subjects of scientific interest even to the
Greeks and Romans, and long before we ourselves were able to read the Egyptian monu-
ments we had at our disposal some communications about them from preserved works of clas-
sical antiquity. Some of these writings belonged to familiar authors like Strabo, Plutarch, Aminianus Marcellus, and some bear un-
familiar names and are uncertain as to origin
and time, like the hieroglyphica of Horapollo
Nilus, and like the traditional book of oriental
priestly wisdom bearing the godly name
Hermes Trismegistos. From these sources
we learn that the vulture was a symbol of
motherhood because it was thought that this
species of birds had only female vultures and
no males.[6] The natural history of the ancients
shows a counterpart to this limitation among
the scarebæus beetles which were revered by
the Egyptians as godly, no females were supposed to exist.[7]

---

[6] "γῦπα δὲ ἄρρενα οὐ φασιγένεσθαι ποτε, ἀιλὰ θηλείας ἀπάσας,"
cited by v. Römer. Über die androgynische Idee des Lebens,
Jahrb. f. Sexuelle Zwischenstufen, V, 1903, p. 732.
[7] Plutarch: Veluti scarabaeos mares tantum esse putarunt
Aegyptii sic inter vultures mares non inveniri statuerunt.

But how does impregnation take place in vultures if only females exist? This is fully answered in a passage of Hórapollo.[8] At a certain time these birds stop in the midst of their flight, open their vagina and are impregnated by the wind.

Unexpectedly we have now reached a point where we can take something as quite probable which only shortly before we had to reject as absurd. It is quite possible that Leonardo was well acquainted with the scientific fable, according to which the Egyptians represented the idea of mother with the picture of the vulture. He was an omnivorous reader whose interest comprised all spheres of literature and knowledge. In the Codex Atlanticus we find an index of all books which he possessed at a certain time,[9] as well as numerous notices about other books which he borrowed from friends, and according to the excerpts which Fr. Richter[10] compiled from his drawings we can

---

[8] Horapollinis Niloi Hieroglyphica edidit Conradus Leemans Amstelodami, 1835. The words referring to the sex of the vulture read as follows (p. 14): "μητέρα μὲν ἐπειδὴ ἄρρεν ἐν τούτῳ γένει τῶν ζώων οὐχ ὑπάρχει."

[9] E. Múntz, l. c., p. 282.   [10] E. Müntz, l. c.

hardly overestimate the extent of his reading. Among these books there was no lack of older as well as contemporary works treating of natural history. All these books were already in print at that time, and it so happens that Milan was the principal place of the young art of book printing in Italy.

When we proceed further we come upon a communication which may raise to a certainty the probability that Leonardo knew the vulture fable. The erudite editor and commentator of Horapollo remarked in connection with the text (p. 172) cited before: *Caeterum hanc fabulam de vulturibus cupide amplexi sunt Patres Ecclesiastici, ut ita argumento ex rerum natura petito refutarent eos, qui Virginis partum negabant; itaque apud omnes fere hujus rei mentio occurit.*

Hence the fable of the monosexuality and the conception of the vulture by no means remained as an indifferent anecdote as in the case of the analogous fable of the scarebæus beetles; that church fathers mastered it in order to have it ready as an argument from natural history against those who doubted the sacred history.

If according the best information from antiquity the vultures were directed to let themselves be impregnated by the wind, why should the same thing not have happened even once in a human female? On account of this use the church fathers were "almost all" in the habit of relating this vulture fable, and now it can hardly remain doubtful that it also became known to Leonardo through so powerful a source.

The origin of Leonardo's vulture phantasy can be conceived in the following manner: While reading in the writings of a church father or in a book on natural science that the vultures are all females and that they know to procreate without the coöperation of a male, a memory emerged in him which became transformed into that phantasy, but which meant to say that he also had been such a vulture child, which had a mother but no father. An echo of pleasure which he experienced at his mother's breast was added to this in the manner as so old impressions alone can manifest themselves. The allusion to the idea of the holy virgin with the child, formed by the authors,

which is so dear to every artist, must have contributed to it to make this phantasy seem to him
valuable and important.   For this helped him
to identify himself with the Christ child, the
comforter and savior of not alone this one
woman.

When we break up an infantile phantasy we
strive to separate the real memory content
from the later motives which modify and distort the same.   In the case of Leonardo we
now think that we know the real content of the
phantasy.   The replacement of the mother by
the vulture indicates that the child missed the
father and felt himself alone with his mother.
The fact of Leonardo's illegitimate birth fits in
with his vulture phantasy; only on account of it
was he able to compare himself with a vulture
child.   But we have discovered as the next
definite fact from his youth that at the age of
five years he had already been received in his
father's home; when this took place, whether a
few months following his birth, or a few weeks
before the taking of the assessment of taxes, is
entirely unknown to us.   The interpretation of
the vulture phantasy then steps in and wants

to tell us that Leonardo did not spend the first decisive years of his life with his father and his step-mother but with his poor, forsaken, real mother, so that he had time to miss his father. This still seems to be a rather meager and rather daring result of the psychoanalytic effort, but on further reflection it will gain in significance. Certainty will be promoted by mentioning the actual relations in Leonardo's childhood. According to the reports, his father Ser Piero da Vinci married the prominent Donna Albiera during the year of Leonardo's birth; it was to the childlessness of this marriage that the boy owed his legalized reception into his father's or rather grandfather's house during his fifth year. However, it is not customary to offer an illegitimate offspring to a young woman's care at the beginning of marriage when she is still expecting to be blessed with children. Years of disappointment must have elapsed before it was decided to adopt the probably handsomely developed illegitimate child as a compensation for legitimate children who were vainly hoped for. It harmonizes best with the interpretation of the vulture-phantasy, if at least three years or perhaps five years of Leonardo's life had elapsed before he changed from his lonely mother to his father's home. But then it had already become too late. In the first three or four years of life impressions are fixed and modes of reactions are formed towards the outer world which can never be robbed of their importance by any later experiences.

If it is true that the incomprehensible childhood reminiscences and the person's phantasies based on them always bring out the most significant of his psychic development, then the fact corroborated by the vulture phantasy, that Leonardo passed the first years of his life alone with his mother must have been a most decisive influence on the formation of his inner life. Under the effect of this constellation it could not have been otherwise than that the child which in his young life encountered one problem more than other children, should have begun to ponder very passionately over this riddle and thus should have become an investigator early in life. For he was tortured by the great questions where do children come from and what has the father to do with their origin. The vague knowledge of this connection between his investigation and his childhood history has later drawn from him the exclamation that it was destined that he should deeply occupy himself with the problem of the bird's flight, for already in his cradle he had been visited by a vulture. To trace the curiosity which is directed to the flight of the bird to the infantile sexual investigation will be a later task which will not be difficult to accomplish.

III

THE element of the vulture represents to us the real memory content in Leonardo's childhood phantasy; the association into which Leonardo himself placed his phantasy threw a bright light on the importance of this content for his later life. In continuing the work of interpretation we now encounter the strange problem why this memory content was elaborated into a homosexual situation. The mother who nursed the child, or rather from whom the child suckled was transformed into a vulture which stuck its tail into the child's mouth. We maintain that the "coda" (tail) of the vulture, following the common substituting usages of language, cannot signify anything else but a male genital or penis. But we do not understand how the phantastic activity came to furnish precisely this maternal bird with the mark of masculinity, and in view of this absurdity we become confused at the possibility of reducing this phantastic structure to rational sense.

However, we must not despair. How many seemingly absurd dreams have we not forced to give up their sense! Why should it become more difficult to accomplish this in a childhood phantasy than in a dream!

Let us remember the fact that it is not good to find one isolated peculiarity, and let us hasten to add another to it which is still more striking.

The vulture-headed goddess *Mut* of the Egyptians, a figure of altogether impersonal character, as expressed by Drexel in Roscher's lexicon, was often fused with other maternal deities of living individuality like Isis and Hathor, but she retained besides her separate existence and reverence. It was especially characteristic of the Egyptian pantheon that the individual gods did not perish in this amalgamation. Besides the composition of deities the simple divine image remained in her independence. In most representations the vulture-headed maternal deity was formed by the

Egyptians in a phallic manner,[1] her body which was distinguished as feminine by its breasts also bore the masculine member in a state of erection.

The goddess Mut thus evinced the same union of maternal and paternal characteristics as in Leonardo's vulture phantasy. Should we explain this concurrence by the assumption that Leonardo knew from studying his book the androgynous nature of the maternal vulture? Such possibility is more than questionable; it seems that the sources accessible to him contained nothing of remarkable determination. It is more likely that here as there the agreement is to be traced to a common, effective and unknown motive.

Mythology can teach us that the androgynous formation, the union of masculine and feminine sex characteristics, did not belong to the goddess Mut alone but also to other deities such as Isis and Hathor, but in the latter perhaps only insofar as they possessed also a motherly nature and became fused with the goddess Mut.[2] It teaches us further that

[1] See the illustrations in Lanzone 1. c. T. CXXXVI-VIII.
[2] v. Römer 1. c.

other Egyptian deities such as Neith of Sais out of whom the Greek Athene was later formed, were originally conceived as androgynous or dihermaphroditic, and that the same held true for many of the Greek gods, especially of the Dionysian circle, as well as for Aphrodite who was later restricted to a feminine love deity. Mythology may also offer the explanation that the phallus which was added to the feminine body was meant to denote the creative primitive force of nature, and that all these hermaphroditic deistic formations express the idea that only a union of the masculine and feminine elements can result in a worthy representation of divine perfection. But none of these observations explain the psychological riddle, namely, that the phantasy of men takes no offense at the fact that a figure which was to embody the essence of the mother should be provided with the mark of the masculine power which is the opposite of motherhood.

The explanation comes from the infantile sexual theories. There really was a time in which the male genital was found to be com-

patible with the representation of the mother.
When the male child first directs his curiosity
to the riddle of the sexual life, he is dominated
by the interest for his own genitals. He finds
this part of the body too valuable and too important to believe that it would be missing in
other persons to whom he feels such a resem-
blance. As he cannot divine that there is still
another equally valuable type of genital formation he must grasp the assumption that all persons, also women, possess such a member as he.
This preconception is so firm in the youthful
investigator that it is not destroyed even by
the first observation of the genitals in little
girls. His perception naturally tells him that
there is something different here than in him,
but he is unable to admit to himself as the content of this perception that he cannot find this
member in girls. That this member may be
missing is to him a dismal and unbearable
thought, and he therefore seeks to reconcile it
by deciding that it also exists in girls but it
is still very small and that it will grow later.[3]

[3] Cf. the observations in the Jahrbuch für Psychoanalytische
und Psychopathologische Forschungen, Vol. I, 1909.

If this expectation does not appear to be fulfilled on later observation he has at his disposal another way of escape. The member also existed in the little girl but it was cut off and on its place there remained a wound. This progress of the theory already makes use of his own painful experience; he was threatened in the meantime that this important organ will be taken away from him if it will form too much of an interest for his occupation. Under the influence of this threat of castration he now interprets his conception of the female genital, henceforth he will tremble for his masculinity, but at the same time he will look with contempt upon those unhappy creatures upon whom, in his opinion, this cruel punishment had already been visited.

Before the child came under the domination of the castration complex, at the time when he still held the woman at her full value, he began to manifest an intensive desire to look as an erotic activity of his impulse. He wished to see the genitals of other persons, originally probably because he wished to compare them with his own. The erotic attraction which emanated from the person of his mother soon reached its height in the longing to see her genital which he believed to be a penis. With the cognition acquired only later that the woman has no penis, this longing often becomes transformed into its opposite and gives place to disgust, which in the years of puberty may become the cause of psychic impotence, of misogyny and of lasting homosexuality. But the fixation on the once so vividly desired object, the penis of the woman, leaves ineradicable traces in the psychic life of the child, which has gone through that fragment of infantile sexual investigation with particular thoroughness. The fetich-like reverence for the feminine foot and shoe seems to take the foot only as a substitutive symbol for the once revered and since then missed member of the woman. The "braid-slashers" without knowing it play the part of persons who perform the act of castration on the female genital.

One will not gain any correct understanding of the activities of the infantile sexuality and probably will consider these communications unworthy of belief, as long as one does not re-

linquish the attitude of our cultural depreciation of the genitals and of the sexual functions
in general. To understand the infantile psychic life one has to look to analogies from
primitive times. For a long series of genera-
tions we have been in the habit of considering
the genitals or *pudenda* as objects of shame,
and in the case of more successful sexual repression as objects of disgust. The majority
of those living to-day only reluctantly obey the
laws of propagation, feeling thereby that their
human dignity is being offended and degraded.
What exists among us of the other conception
of the sexual life is found only in the unculti-
vated and in the lower social strata; among the
higher and more refined types it is concealed as
culturally inferior, and its activity is ventured
only under the embittered admonition of a
guilty conscience. It was quite different in
the primitive times of the human race. From
the laborious collections of students of civiliza-
tion one gains the conviction that the genitals
were originally the pride and hope of living beings, they enjoyed divine worship, and the
divine nature of their functions was trans-

ported to all newly acquired activities of mankind. Through sublimation of its essential elements there arose innumerable god-figures, and at the time when the relation of official religions with sexual activity was already hidden from the general consciousness, secret cults labored to preserve it alive among a number of the initiated. In the course of cultural development it finally happened that so much godliness and holiness had been extracted from sexuality that the exhausted remnant fell into contempt. But considering the indestructibility which is in the nature of all psychic impressions one need not wonder that even the most primitive forms of genital worship could be demonstrated until quite recent times, and that language, customs and superstitions of present day humanity contain the remnants of all phases of this course of development.[4]

Important biological analogies have taught us that the psychic development of the individual is a short repetition of the course of development of the race, and we shall therefore not find improbable what the psychoanalytic in-

[4] Cf. Richard Payne Knight: The Cult of Priapus.

vestigation of the child's psyche asserts concerning the infantile estimation of the genitals. The infantile assumption of the maternal penis is thus the common source of origin for the androgynous formation of the maternal deities like the Egyptian goddess Mut and the vulture's "coda" (tail) in Leonardo's childhood phantasy. As a matter of fact, it is only through misunderstanding that these deistic representations are designated hermaphroditic in the medical sense of the word.   In none of them is there a union of the true genitals of both sexes as they are united in some deformed beings to the disgust of every human eye; but besides the breast as a mark of motherhood there is also the male member, just as it existed in the first imagination of the child about his mother's body.   Mythology has retained for the faithful this revered and very early fancied bodily formation of the mother.   The prominence given to the vulture-tail in Leonardo's phantasy we can now translate as follows: At that time when I directed my tender curiosity to my mother I still adjudged to her a genital like my own.   A further testimonial of Leonardo's precocious sexual investigation, which in our opinion became decisive for his entire life.

A brief reflection now admonishes us that we should not be satisfied with the explanation of the vulture-tail in Leonardo's childhood phantasy. It seems as if it contained more than we as yet understand. For its more striking feature really consisted in the fact that the nursing at the mother's breast was transformed into being nursed, that is into a passive act which thus gives the situation an undoubted homosexual character. Mindful of the historical probability that Leonardo behaved in life as a homosexual in feeling, the question obtrudes itself whether this phantasy does not point to a causal connection between Leonardo's childhood relations to his mother and the later manifest, if only ideal, homosexuality. We would not venture to draw such conclusion from Leonardo's disfigured reminiscence were it not for the fact that we know from our psychoanalytic investigation of homosexual patients that such a relation exists, indeed it really is an intimate and necessary relation.

Homosexual men who have started in our times an energetic action against the legal limitations of their sexual activity are fond of representing themselves through theoretical spokesmen as evincing a sexual variation, which may be distinguished from the very beginning, as an intermediate stage of sex or as "a third sex." In other words, they maintain that they are men who are forced by organic determinants originating in the germ to find that pleasure in the man which they cannot feel in the woman. As much as one would wish to subscribe to their demands out of humane considerations, one must nevertheless exercise reserve regarding their theories which were formulated without regard for the psychic genesis of homosexuality. Psychoanalysis offers the means to fill this gap and to put to test the assertions of the homosexuals. It is true that psychoanalysis fulfilled this task in only a small number of people, but all investigation thus far undertaken brought the same surprising results.[5] In all our male homosexuals

[5] Prominently among those who undertook these investigations are I. Sadger, whose results I can essentially corroborate

there was a very intensive erotic attachment to a feminine person, as a rule to the mother, which was manifest in the very first period of childhood and later entirely forgotten by the individual. This attachment was produced or favored by too much love from the mother herself, but was also furthered by the retirement or absence of the father during the childhood period. Sadger emphasizes the fact that the mothers of his homosexual patients were often man-women, or women with energetic traits of character who were able to crowd out the father from the place allotted to him in the family. I have sometimes observed the same thing, but I was more impressed by those cases in which the father was absent from the beginning or disappeared early so that the boy was altogether under feminine influence. It almost seems that the presence of a strong father would assure for the son the proper decision in the selection of his object from the opposite sex.

from my own experience. I am also aware that Stekel of Vienna, Ferenczi of Budapest, and Brill of New York, came to the same conclusions.

Following this primary stage, a transformation takes place whose mechanisms we know but whose motive forces we have not yet grasped. The love of the mother cannot continue to develop consciously so that it merges into repression. The boy represses the love for the mother by putting himself in her place, by identifying himself with her, and by taking his own person as a model through the similarity of which he is guided in the selection of his love object. He thus becomes homosexual; as a matter of fact he returns to the stage of autoerotism, for the boys whom the growing adult now loves are only substitutive persons or revivals of his own childish person, whom he loves in the same way as his mother loved him. We say that he finds his love object on the road to narcism, for the Greek legend called a boy Narcissus to whom nothing was more pleasing than his own mirrored image, and who became transformed into a beautiful flower of this name.

Deeper psychological discussions justify the assertion that the person who becomes homosexual in this manner remains fixed in his un-

conscious on the memory picture or his mother.
By repressing the love for his mother he con-
serves the same in his unconscious and henceforth remains faithful to her. When as a
lover he seems to pursue boys, he really thus
runs away from women who could cause him
to become faithless to his mother. Through
direct observation of individual cases we could
demonstrate that he who is seemingly receptive
only of masculine stimuli is in reality influenced
by the charms emanating from women just like
a normal person, but each and every time he
hastens to transfer the stimulus he received
from the woman to a male object and in this
manner he repeats again and again the mechanism through which he acquired his homosexuality.

It is far from us to exaggerate the importance of these explanations concerning the
psychic genesis of homosexuality. It is quite
clear that they are in crass opposition to the
official theories of the homosexual spokesmen,
but we are aware that these explanations are
not sufficiently comprehensive to render possible a final explanation of the problem. What

one\ calls homosexual for practical purposes
may have its origin in a variety of psychosexual inhibiting processes, and the process recognized by us is perhaps only one among many,
and has reference only to one type of "homosexuality." We must also admit, that the
number of cases in our homosexual type which
shows the conditions required by us, exceeds by
far those cases in which the resulting effect
really appears, so that even we cannot reject
the supposed coöperation of unknown constitutional factors from which one was otherwise
wont to deduce the whole of homosexuality.
As a matter of fact there would be no occasion
for entering into the psychic genesis of the
form of homosexuality studied by us if there
were not a strong presumption that Leonardo,
from whose vulture-phantasy we started, really
belonged to this one type of homosexuality.

As little as is known concerning the sexual
behavior of the great artist and investigator,
we must still trust to the probability that the
testimonies of his contemporaries did not go
far astray. In the light of this tradition he appears to us as a man whose sexual need and

activity were extraordinarily low, as if a higher striving had raised him above the common animal need of mankind. It may be open to doubt whether he ever sought direct sexual gratification, and in what manner, or whether he could dispense with it altogether. We are justified, however, to look also in him for those emotional streams which imperatively force others to the sexual act, for we cannot imagine a human psychic life in whose development the sexual desire in the broadest sense, the libido, has not had its share, whether the latter has withdrawn itself far from the original aim or whether it was detained from being put into execution.

Anything but traces of unchanged sexual desire we need not expect in Leonardo. These point however to one direction and allow us to count him among homosexuals. It has always been emphasized that he took as his pupils only strikingly handsome boys and youths. He was kind and considerate towards them, he cared for them and nursed them himself when they were ill, just like a mother nurses her children, as his own mother might have cared for

him.   As he selected them on account of their
beauty rather than their talent, none of them
—Cesare da Sesto, G. Boltraffio, Andrea Salaino, Francesco Melzi and the others—ever
became a prominent artist.   Most of them
could not make themselves independent of their
master and disappeared after his death without
leaving a more definite physiognomy to the history of art.   The others who by their productions earned the right to call themselves his
pupils, as Luini and Bazzi, nicknamed Sodoma,
he probably did not know personally.

   We realize that we will have to face the ob-
jection that Leonardo's behavior towards his
pupils surely had nothing to do with sexual
motives, and permits no conclusion as to his
sexual peculiarity.   Against this we wish to
assert with all caution that our conception ex-
plains some strange features in the master's behavior which otherwise would have remained
enigmatical.   Leonardo kept a diary; he made
entries in his small hand, written from right to
left which were meant only for himself.   It is
to be noted that in this diary he addressed himself with "thou": "Learn from master Lucca

the multiplication of roots."[6] "Let master d'Abacco show thee the square of the circle."[7] Or on the occasion of a journey he entered in his diary:

"I am going to Milan to look after the affairs of my garden . . . order two pack-sacks to be made. Ask Boltraffio to show thee his turning-lathe and let him polish a stone on it.—Leave the book to master Andrea il Todesco."[8] Or he wrote a resolution of quite different significance: "Thou must show in thy treatise that the earth is a star, like the moon or resembling it, and thus prove the nobility of our world."[9]

In this diary, which like the diaries of other mortals often skim over the most important events of the day with only few words or ignore them altogether, one finds a few entries which on account of their peculiarity are cited

[6] Edm. Solmi: Leonardo da Vinci, German translation, p. 152.

[7] Solmi, l. c. p. 203.

[8] Leonardo thus behaves like one who was in the habit of making a daily confession to another person whom he now replaced by his diary. For an assumption as to who this person may have been see Merejkowski, p. 309.

[9] M. Herzfeld: Leonardo da Vinci, 1906, p. 141.

by all of Leonardo's biographers. They show
notations referring to the master's petty expenses, which are recorded with painful ex-
actitude as if coming from a pedantic and
strictly parsimonious family father, while there
is nothing to show that he spent greater sums,
or that the artist was well versed in household
management. One of these notes refers to a
new cloak which he bought for his pupil
Andrea Salaino: [10]

Silver brocade	Lira	15	Soldi	4
Crimson velvet for trimming ..	"	9	"	0
Braid	"	0	"	9
Buttons	"	0	"	12

Another very detailed notice gives all the expenses which he incurred through the bad qual-
ities and the thieving tendencies of another
pupil or model: "On 21st day of April, 1490,
I started this book and started again the
horse.[11] Jacomo came to me on Magdalene
day, 1490, at the age of ten years (marginal
note: thievish, mendacious, willful, glutton-
ous). On the second day I ordered for him

---

[10] The wording is that of Merejkowski, l. c. p. 237.
[11] The equestrian monument of Francesco Sforza.

two shirts, a pair of pants, and a jacket, and as I put the money away to pay for the things named he stole the money from my purse, and it was never possible to make him confess, although I was absolutely sure of it (marginal note: 4 Lira . . .)." So the report continues concerning the misdeeds of the little boy and concludes with the expense account: "In the first year, a cloak, Lira 2: 6 shirts, Lira 4: 3 jackets, Lira 6: 4 pair of socks, Lira 7, etc." [12]

Leonardo's biographers, to whom nothing was further than to solve the riddle in the psychic life of their hero from these slight weaknesses and peculiarities, were wont to remark in connection with these peculiar accounts that they emphasized the kindness and consideration of the master for his pupils. They forget thereby that it is not Leonardo's behavior that needs an explanation, but the fact that he left us these testimonies of it. As it is impossible to ascribe to him the motive of smuggling into our hands proofs of his kindness, we must assume that another affective motive caused him to write this down. It is not easy to con-

[12] The full wording is found in M. Herzfeld, 1. c. p. 45.

jecture what this motive was, and we could not
give any if not for another account found
among Leonardo's papers which throws a bril-
liant light on these peculiarly petty notices
about his pupils' clothes, and others of a
kind: [13]

Burial expenses following the death of
    Caterina ....27 florins
  2 pounds wax ....18 "
  Cataphalc ....12 "
  For the transportation and erection of
    the cross .... 4 "
  Pall bearers .... 8 "
  To 4 priests and 4 clerics ....20 "
  Ringing of bells .... 2 "
  To grave diggers ....16 "
  For the approval—to the officials..... 1 "

          To sum up ....108 florins

Previous expenses:
  To the doctor ....4 florins
  For sugar and candles .. 12 "

                 16 florins

        Sum total ....124 florins

[13] Merejkowski l. c.—As a disappointing illustration of the
vagueness of the information concerning Leonardo's intimate

The writer Merejkowski is the only one who can tell us who this Caterina was. From two different short notices he concludes that she was the mother of Leonardo, the poor peasant woman from Vinci, who came to Milan in 1493 to visit her son then 41 years old. .While on this visit she fell ill and was taken to the hospital by Leonardo, and following her death she was buried by her son with such sumptuous funeral.[14]

This deduction of the psychological writer of romances is not capable of proof, but it can lay claim to so many inner probabilities, it agrees so well with everything we know besides about Leonardo's emotional activity that I cannot refrain from accepting it as correct. Leonardo succeeded in forcing his feelings under the yoke

life, meager as it is, I mention the fact that the same expense account is given by Solmi with considerable variation (German translation, p. 104). The most serious difference is the substitution of florins by soldi. One may assume that in this account florins do not mean the old "gold florins," but those used at a later period which amounted to 1⅔ lira or 33½ soldi.— Solmi represents Caterina as a servant who had taken care of Leonardo's household for a certain time. The source from which the two representations of this account were taken was not accessible to me.

[14] "Caterina came in July, 1493."

of investigation and in inhibiting their free utterance, but even in him there were episodes in
which the suppression obtained expression, and
one of these was the death of his mother whom
he once loved so ardently. Through this account of the burial expenses he represents to us
the mourning of his mother in an almost un-
recognizable distortion. We wonder how such
a distortion could have come about, and we certainly cannot grasp it when viewed under normal mental processes. But similar mechanisms are familiar to us under the abnormal
conditions of neuroses, and especially in the so-
called *compulsion neurosis*. Here one can ob-
serve how the expressions of more intensive
feelings have been displaced to trivial and even
foolish performances. The opposing forces
succeeded in debasing the expression of these
repressed feelings to such an extent that one is
forced to estimate the intensity of these feelings as extremely unimportant, but the imperative compulsion with which these insignificant
acts express themselves betrays the real force
of the feelings which are rooted in the unconscious, which consciousness would wish to dis-

avow. Only by bearing in mind the mechanisms of compulsion neurosis can one explain
Leonardo's account of the funeral expenses of
his mother. In his unconscious he was still
tied to her as in childhood, by erotically tinged
feelings; the opposition of the repression of
this childhood love which appeared later stood
in the way of erecting to her in his diary a
different and more dignified monument, but
what resulted as a compromise of this neurotic
conflict had to be put in operation and hence
the account was entered in the diary which thus
came to the knowledge of posterity as something incomprehensible.

It is not venturing far to transfer the interpretation obtained from the funeral expenses to the accounts dealing with his pupils.
Accordingly we would say that here also we
deal with a case in which Leonardo's meager
remnants of libidinous feelings compulsively
obtained a distorted expression. The mother
and the pupils, the very images of his own boy-
ish beauty, would be his sexual objects—as far
as his sexual repression dominating his nature
would allow such manifestations—and the

compulsion to note with painful circumstantiality his expenses on their behalf, would designate the strange betrayal of his rudimentary conflicts. From this we would conclude that Leonardo's love-life really belonged to that type of homosexuality, the psychic development of which we were able to disclose, and the appearance of the homosexual situation in his vulture-phantasy would become comprehensible to us, for it states nothing more or less than what we have asserted before concerning that type. It requires the following interpretation: Through the erotic relations to my mother I became a homosexual.[15]

[15] The manner of expression through which the repressed libidio could manifest itself in Leonardo, such as circumstantiality and marked interest in money, belongs to those traits of character which emanate from anal eroticism. Cf. Character und Analerotik in the second series of my Sammlung zur Neurosenlehre, 1909, also Brill's Psychoanalysis, its Theories and Practical Applications, Chap. XIII, Anal Eroticism and Character, Saunders, Philadelphia.

IV

THE vulture phantasy of Leonardo still absorbs our interest. In words which only too plainly recall a sexual act ("and has many times struck against my lips with his tail"), Leonardo emphasizes the intensity of the erotic relations between the mother and the child. A second memory content of the phantasy can readily be conjectured from the association of the activity of the mother (of the vulture) with the accentuation of the mouth zone. We can translate it as follows: My mother has pressed on my mouth innumerable passionate kisses. The phantasy is composed of the memories of being nursed and of being kissed by the mother.

A kindly nature has bestowed upon the artist the capacity to express in artistic productions his most secret psychic feelings hidden even to himself, which powerfully affect outsiders who

78

MONA LISA

are strangers to the artist without their being able to state whence this emotivity comes. Should there be no evidence in Leonardo's work of that which his memory retained as the strongest impression of his childhood? One would have to expect it. However, when one considers what profound transformations an impression of an artist has to experience before it can add its contribution to the work of art, one is obliged to moderate considerably his expectation of demonstrating something definite. This is especially true in the case of Leonardo.

He who thinks of Leonardo's paintings will be reminded by the remarkably fascinating and puzzling smile which he enchanted on the lips of all his feminine figures. It is a fixed smile on elongated, sinuous lips which is considered characteristic of him and is preferentially designated as "Leonardesque." In the singular and beautiful visage of the Florentine Monna Lisa del Giocondo it has produced the greatest effect on the spectators and even perplexed them. This smile was in need of an interpretation, and received many of the most varied kind but none of them was considered satisfactory. As Gruyer puts it: "It is almost four centuries since Monna Lisa causes all those to lose their heads who have looked upon her for some time." [1]

Muther states: [2] "What fascinates the spectator is the demoniacal charm of this smile. Hundreds of poets and writers have written about this woman, who now seems to smile upon us seductively and now to stare coldly and lifelessly into space, but nobody has solved the riddle of her smile, nobody has interpreted her thoughts. Everything, even the scenery is mysterious and dream-like, trembling as if in the sultriness of sensuality."

The idea that two diverse elements were united in the smile of Monna Lisa has been felt by many critics. They therefore recognize in the play of features of the beautiful Florentine lady the most perfect representation of the contrasts dominating the love-life of the woman which is foreign to man, as that of reserve and seduction, and of most devoted tenderness and inconsiderateness in urgent and

[1] Seidlitz: Leonardo da Vinci, II Bd., p. 280.
[2] Geschichte der Malerei, Bd. I, p. 314.

consuming sensuality. Müntz [3] expresses himself in this manner: "One knows what indecipherable and fascinating enigma Monna Lisa Gioconda has been putting for nearly four centuries to the admirers who crowd around her. No artist (I borrow the expression of the delicate writer who hides himself under the pseudonym of Pierre de Corlay) has ever translated in this manner the very essence of femininity: the tenderness and coquetry, the modesty and quiet voluptuousness, the whole mystery of the heart which holds itself aloof, of a brain which reflects, and of a personality who watches itself and yields nothing from herself except radiance. . . ." The Italian Angelo Conti [4] saw the picture in the Louvre illumined by a ray of the sun and expressed himself as follows: "The woman smiled with a royal calmness, her instincts of conquest, of ferocity, the entire heredity of the species, the will of seduction and ensnaring, the charm of the deceiver, the kindness which conceals a

[3] l. c. p. 417.
[4] A. Conti: Leonardo pittore, Conferenze Fiorentine, l. c. p. 93.

cruel purpose, all that appears and disappears alternately behind the laughing veil and melts into the poem of her smile. . . . Good and evil, cruelty and compassion, graceful and cat-like, she laughed. . . ."

Leonardo painted this picture four years, perhaps from 1503 until 1507, during his second sojourn in Florence when he was about the age of fifty years.   According to Vasari he applied the choicest artifices in order to divert the lady during the sittings and to hold that smile firmly on her features.   Of all the graceful-ness that his brush reproduced on the canvas at that time the picture preserves but very lit-tle in its present state.   During its production it was considered the highest that art could accomplish; it is certain, however, that it did not satisfy Leonardo himself, that he pro-nounced it as unfinished and did not deliver it to the one who ordered it, but took it with him to France where his benefactor Francis I, ac-quired it for the Louvre.

Let us leave the physiognomic riddle of Monna Lisa unsolved, and let us note the un-equivocal fact that her smile fascinated the artist no less than all the spectators for these 400 years. This captivating smile had thereafter returned in all of his pictures and in those of his pupils. As Leonardo's Monna Lisa was a portrait we cannot assume that he has added to her face a trait of his own so difficult to express which she herself did not possess. It seems, we cannot help but believe, that he found this smile in his model and became so charmed by it that from now on he endowed it on all the free creations of his phantasy. This obvious conception is, e.g., expressed by A. Konstantinowa in the following manner: [5]

"During the long period in which the master occupied himself with the portrait of Monna Lisa del Gioconda, he entered into the physiognomic delicacies of this feminine face with such sympathy of feeling that he transferred these creatures, especially the mysterious smile and the peculiar glance, to all faces which he later painted or drew. The mimic peculiarity of Gioconda can even be perceived in the picture of John the Baptist in the Louvre. But above all they are distinctly recognized in the

[5] l. c. p. 45.

features of Mary in the picture of St. Anne of the Louvre."

But the case could have been different. The need for a deeper reason for the fascination which the smile of Gioconda exerted on the artist from which he could not rid himself has been felt by more than one of his biographers. W. Pater, who sees in the picture of Monna Lisa the embodiment of the entire erotic experience of modern man, and discourses so excellently on "that unfathomable smile always with a touch of something sinister in it, which plays over all Leonardo's work," leads us to another track when he says: [6]

"Besides, the picture is a portrait. From childhood we see this image defining itself on the fabric of his dream; and but for express historical testimony, we might fancy that this was but his ideal lady, embodied and beheld at last."

Herzfeld surely must have had something similar in mind when stating that in Monna Lisa Leonardo encountered himself and there-

[6] W. Pater: The Renaissance, p. 124, The Macmillan Co., 1910.

fore found it possible to put so much of his own nature into the picture, "whose features from time immemorial have been imbedded with mysterious sympathy in Leonardo's soul." [7]

Let us endeavor to clear up these intimations. It was quite possible that Leonardo was fascinated by the smile of Monna Lisa, because it had awakened something in him which had slumbered in his soul for a long time, in all probability an old memory. This memory was of sufficient importance to stick to him once it had been aroused; he was forced continually to provide it with new expression. The assurance of Pater that we can see an image like that of Monna Lisa defining itself from Leonardo's childhood on the fabric of his dreams, seems worthy of belief and deserves to be taken literally.

Vasari mentions as Leonardo's first artistic endeavors, "heads of women who laugh." [8] The passage, which is beyond suspicion, as it is not meant to prove anything, reads more precisely as follows: [9]   "He formed in his youth

[7] M. Herzfeld: Leonardo da Vinci, p. 88.
[8] Scognamiglio, l. c. p. 32.
[9] L. Schorn, Bd. III, 1843, p. 6.

some laughing feminine heads out of lime,
which have been reproduced in plaster, and
some heads of children, which were as beautiful as if modeled by the hands of a master. . . ."

Thus we discover that his practice of art began with the representation of two kinds of objects, which would perforce remind us of the
two kinds of sexual objects which we have in-
ferred from the analysis of his vulture phantasy. If the beautiful children's heads were
reproductions of his own childish person, then
the laughing women were nothing else but reproductions of Caterina, his mother, and we
are beginning to have an inkling of the possibility that his mother possessed that mysterious smile which he lost, and which fascinated
him so much when he found it again in the
Florentine lady.[10]

The painting of Leonardo which in point
of time stands nearest to the Monna Lisa is

[10] The same is assumed by Merejkowski, who imagined a
childhood for Leonardo which deviates in the essential points
from ours, drawn from the results of the vulture phantasy.
But if Leonardo himself had displayed this smile, tradition
hardly would have failed to report to us this coincidence.

SAINT ANNE

the so-called Saint Anne of the Louvre, representing Saint Anne, Mary and the Christ child. It shows the Leonardesque smile most beautifully portrayed in the two feminine heads. It is impossible to find out how much earlier or later than the portrait of Monna Lisa Leonardo began to paint this picture. As both works extended over years, we may well assume that they occupied the master simultaneously. But it would best harmonize with our expectation if precisely the absorption in the features of Monna Lisa would have instigated Leonardo to form the composition of Saint Anne from his phantasy. For if the smile of Gioconda had conjured up in him the memory of his mother, we would naturally understand that he was first urged to produce a glorification of motherhood, and to give back to her the smile he found in that prominent lady. We may thus allow our interest to glide over from the portrait of Monna Lisa to this other hardly less beautiful picture, now also in the Louvre.

Saint Anne with the daughter and grandchild is a subject seldom treated in the Italian art of painting; at all events Leonardo's representation differs widely from all that is otherwise known.   Muther states: [11]

"Some masters like Hans Fries, the older Holbein, and Girolamo dei Libri, made Anne sit near Mary and placed the child between the two.   Others like Jakob Cornelicz in his Berlin pictures, represented Saint Anne as holding in her arm the small figure of Mary upon which sits the still smaller figure of the Christ child." In Leonardo's picture Mary sits on her mother's lap, bent forward and is stretching out both arms after the boy who plays with a little lamb, and must have slightly maltreated it. The grandmother has one of her unconcealed arms propped on her hip and looks down on both with a blissful smile.   The grouping is certainly not quite unconstrained.   But the smile which is playing on the lips of both women, although unmistakably the same as in the picture of Monna Lisa, has lost its sinister and mysterious character; it expresses a calm blissfulness.[12]

[11] l. c. p. 309.
[12] A. Konstantinowa, l. c., says: "Mary looks tenderly down on her beloved child with a smile that recalls the mysterious expression of la Gioconda." Elsewhere speaking of

On becoming somewhat engrossed in this picture it suddenly dawns upon the spectator that only Leonardo could have painted this picture, as only he could have formed the vulture phantasy. This picture contains the synthesis of the history of Leonardo's childhood, the details of which are explainable by the most intimate impressions of his life. In his father's home he found not only the kind step-mother Donna Albiera, but also the grandmother, his father's mother, Monna Lucia, who we will assume was not less tender to him than grandmothers are wont to be. This circumstance must have furnished him with the facts for the representation of a childhood guarded by a mother and grandmother. Another striking feature of the picture assumes still greater significance. Saint Anne, the mother of Mary and the grandmother of the boy who must have been a matron, is formed here perhaps somewhat more mature and more serious than Saint Mary, but still as a young woman of unfaded beauty. As a matter of fact Leonardo gave

Mary she says: "The smile of Gioconda floats upon her features."

the boy two mothers, the one who stretched out her arms after him and another who is seen in the background, both are represented with the blissful smile of maternal happiness. This peculiarity of the picture has not failed to excite the wonder of the authors. Muther, for instance, believes that Leonardo could not bring himself to paint old age, folds and wrinkles, and therefore formed also Anne as a woman of radiant beauty. Whether one can be satisfied with this explanation is a question. Other writers have taken occasion to deny generally the sameness of age of mother and daughter.[13] However, Muther's tentative explanation is sufficient proof for the fact that the impression of Saint Anne's youthful appearance was furnished by the picture and is not an imagination produced by a tendency.

Leonardo's childhood was precisely as remarkable as this picture. He has had two mothers, the first his true mother, Caterina, from whom he was torn away between the age of three and five years, and a young tender step-mother, Donna Albiera, his father's wife.

[13] Cf. v. Seidlitz, l. c. Bd. II, p. 274.

By connecting this fact of his childhood with the one mentioned above and condensing them into a uniform fusion, the composition of Saint Anne, Mary and the Child, formed itself in him. The maternal form further away from the boy designated as grandmother, corresponds in appearance and in spatial relation to the boy, with the real first mother, Caterina. With the blissful smile of Saint Anne the artist actually disavowed and concealed the envy which the unfortunate mother felt when she was forced to give up her son to her more aristocratic rival, as once before her lover.

Our feeling that the smile of Monna Lisa del Gioconda awakened in the man the memory of the mother of his first years of childhood would thus be confirmed from another work of Leonardo. Following the production of Monna Lisa, Italian artists depicted in Madonnas and prominent ladies the humble dipping of the head and the peculiar blissful smile of the poor peasant girl Caterina, who brought to the world the noble son who was destined to paint, investigate, and suffer.

When Leonardo succeeded in reproducing in

the face of Monna Lisa the double sense comprised in this smile, namely, the promise of unlimited tenderness, and sinister threat (in the words of Pater), he remained true even in this to the content of his earliest reminiscence. For the love of the mother became his destiny, it determined his fate and the privations which were in store for him. The impetuosity of the caressing to which the vulture phantasy points was only too natural. The poor forsaken mother had to give vent through mother's love to all her memories of love enjoyed as well as to all her yearnings for more affection; she was forced to it, not only in order to compensate herself for not having a husband, but also the child for not having a father who wanted to love it. In the manner of all ungratified mothers she thus took her little son in place of her husband, and robbed him of a part of his virility by the too early maturing of his eroticism. The love of the mother for the suckling whom she nourishes and cares for is something far deeper reaching than her later affection for the growing child. It is of the nature of a fully gratified love affair, which fulfills not only all the psychic wishes but also all physical needs, and when it represents one of the forms of happiness attainable by man it is due, in no little measure, to the possibility of gratifying without reproach also wish feelings which were long repressed and designated as perverse.[14] Even in the happiest recent marriage the father feels that his child, especially the little boy has become his rival, and this gives origin to an antagonism against the favorite one which is deeply rooted in the unconscious.

When in the prime of his life Leonardo re-encountered that blissful and ecstatic smile as it had once encircled his mother's mouth in caressing, he had long been under the ban of an inhibition, forbidding him ever again to desire such tenderness from women's lips. But as he had become a painter he endeavored to reproduce this smile with his brush and furnish all his pictures with it, whether he executed them himself or whether they were done by his pupils under his direction, as in Leda,

[14] Cf. Three Contributions to the Theory of Sex, translated by A. A. Brill, 2nd edition, 1916, Monograph series.

John, and Bacchus. The latter two are variations of the same type. Muther says: "From the locust eater of the Bible Leonardo made a Bacchus, an Apollo, who with a mysterious smile on his lips, and with his soft thighs crossed, looks on us with infatuated eyes." These pictures breathe a mysticism into the secret of which one dares not penetrate; at most one can make the effort to construct the connection to Leonardo's earlier productions. The figures are again androgynous but no longer in the sense of the vulture phantasy, they are pretty boys of feminine tenderness with feminine forms; they do not cast down their eyes but gaze mysteriously triumphant, as if they knew of a great happy issue concerning which one must remain quiet; the familiar fascinating smile leads us to infer that it is a love secret. It is possible that in these forms Leonardo disavowed and artistically conquered the unhappiness of his love life, in that he represented the wish fulfillment of the boy infatuated with his mother in such blissful union of the male and female nature.

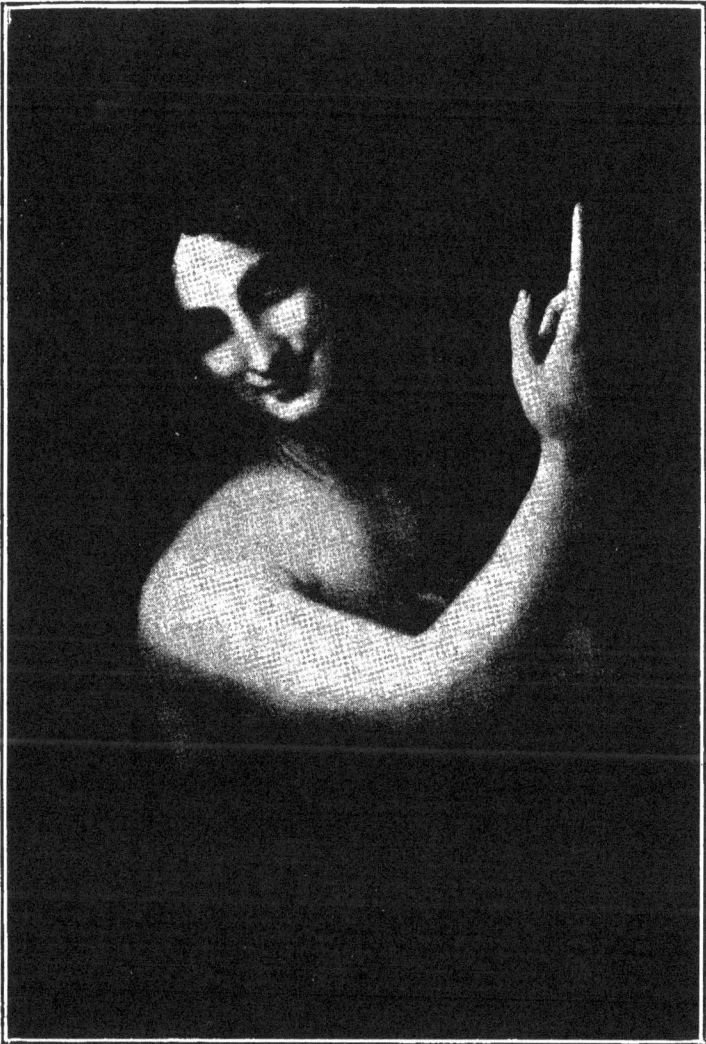

JOHN THE BAPTIST

V

AMONG the entries in Leonardo's diaries there is one which absorbs the reader's attention through its important content and on account of a small formal error. In July, 1504, he wrote:

"Adi 9 Luglio, 1504, mercoledi, a ore 7 mori Ser Piero da Vinci notalio al palazzo del Potestà, mio padre, a ore 7. Era d'età d'anni 80, lasciò 10 figlioli maschi e 2 feminine." [1]

The notice as we see deals with the death of Leonardo's father. The slight error in its form consists in the fact that in the computation of the time "at 7 o'clock" is repeated two times, as if Leonardo had forgotten at the end of the sentence that he had already written it at the beginning. It is only a triviality to

[1] "On the 9th of July, 1504, Wednesday at 7 o'clock died Ser Piero da Vinci, notary at the palace of the Podesta, my father, at 7 o'clock. He was 80 years old, left 10 sons and 2 daughters." (E. Müntz, l. c. p. 13.)

which any one but a psychoanalyst would pay no attention. Perhaps he would not even notice it, or if his attention would be called to it he would say "that can happen to anybody during absent-mindedness or in an affective state and has no further meaning."

The psychoanalyst thinks differently; to him nothing is too trifling as a manifestation of hidden psychic processes; he has long learned that such forgetting or repetition is full of meaning, and that one is indebted to the "absent-mindedness" when it makes possible the betrayal of otherwise concealed feelings.

We would say that, like the funeral account of Caterina and the expense account of the pupils, this notice, too, corresponds to a case in which Leonardo was unsuccessful in suppressing his affects, and the long hidden feeling forcibly obtained a distorted expression.   Also the form is similar, it shows the same pedantic precisión, the same pushing forward of numbers.[2]

We call such a repetition a perseveration.

[2] I shall overlook a greater error committed by Leonardo in his notice in that he gives his 77-year-old father 80 years.

It is an excellent means to indicate the affective accentuation. One recalls for example Saint Peter's angry speech against his unworthy representative on earth, as given in Dante's Paradiso: [3]

> "Quegli ch'usurpa in terra il luoga mio
> Il luoga mio, il luogo mio, che vaca
> Nella presenza del Figliuol di Dio,
> Fatto ha del cimiterio mio cloaca."

Without Leonardo's affective inhibition the entry into the diary could perhaps have read as follows: To-day at 7 o'clock died my father, Ser Piero da Vinci, my poor father! But the displacement of the perseveration to the most indifferent determination of the obituary to dying-hour robs the notice of all pathos and lets us recognize that there was something here to conceal and to suppress.

Ser Piero da Vinci, notary and descendant of notaries, was a man of great energy who attained respect and affluence. He was married four times, the two first wives died childless,

[3] "He who usurps on earth my place, my place, my place, which is void in the presence of the Son of God, has made out of my cemetery a sewer." Canto XXXVII.

and not till the third marriage has he gotten the first legitimate son, in 1476, when Leonardo was 24 years old, and had long ago changed his father's home for the studio of his master Verrocchio. With the fourth and last wife whom he married when he was already in the fifties he begot nine sons and two daughters.[4]

To be sure the father also assumed importance in Leonardo's psychosexual development, and what is more, it was not only in a negative sense, through his absence during the boy's first childhood years, but also directly through his presence in his later childhood. He who as a child desires his mother, cannot help wishing to put himself in his father's place, to identify himself with him in his phantasy and later make it his life's task to triumph over him. As Leonardo was not yet five years old when he was received into his paternal home, the young step-mother, Albiera, certainly must have taken the place of his mother in his feeling, and this brought him into that relation of

---

[4] It seems that in that passage of the diary Leonardo also erred in the number of his sisters and brothers, which stands in remarkable contrast to the apparent exactness of the same.

rivalry to his father which may be designated as normal. As is known, the preference for homosexuality did not manifest itself till near the years of puberty. When Leonardo accepted this preference the identification with the father lost all significance for his sexual life, but continued in other spheres of nonerotic activity. We hear that he was fond of luxury and pretty raiments, and kept servants and horses, although according to Vasari's words "he hardly possessed anything and worked little." We shall not hold his artistic taste entirely responsible for all these special likings; we recognize in them also the compulsion to copy his father and to excel him. He played the part of the great gentleman to the poor peasant girl, hence the son retained the incentive that he also play the great gentleman, he had the strong feeling "to out-herod Herod," and to show his father exactly how the real high rank looks.

Whoever works as an artist certainly feels as a father to his works. The identification with his father had a fateful result in Leonardo's works of art. He created them and then troubled himself no longer about them, just as his father did not trouble himself about him. The later worriments of his father could change nothing in this compulsion, as the latter originated from the impressions of the first years of childhood, and the repression having remained unconscious was incorrigible through later experiences.

At the time of the Renaissance, and even much later, every artist was in need of a gentleman of rank to act as his benefactor. This patron was wont to give the artist commissions for work and entirely controlled his destiny. Leonardo found his patron in Lodovico Sforza, nicknamed Il Moro, a man of high aspirations, ostentations, diplomatically astute, but of an unstable and unreliable character. In his court in Milan, Leonardo spent the best period of his life, while in his service he evinced his most uninhibited productive activity as is evidenced in The Last Supper, and in the equestrian statue of Francesco Sforza. He left Milan before the catastrophe struck Lodovico Moro, who died a prisoner in a French prison. When the news of his benefactor's fate reached

Leonardo he made the following entry in his diary: "The duke has lost state, wealth, and liberty, not one of his works will be finished by himself."[5] It is remarkable and surely not without significance that he here raises the same reproach to his benefactor that posterity was to apply to him, as if he wanted to lay the responsibility to a person who substituted his father-series, for the fact that he himself left his works unfinished. As a matter of fact he was not wrong in what he said about the Duke.

However, if the imitation of his father hurt him as an artist, his resistance against the father was the infantile determinant of his perhaps equally vast accomplishment as an artist. According to Merejkowski's beautiful comparison he was like a man who awoke too early in the darkness, while the others were all still asleep. He dared utter this bold principle which contains the justification for all independent investigation: *"Chi disputa allegando l'autorità non adopra l'ingegno ma piuttosto la memoria"* (Whoever refers to authorities in disputing ideas, works with his memory rather

[5] v. Seidlitz, l. c., II, p. 270.

than with his reason).⁶   Thus he became the
first modern natural philosopher, and his cour-
age was rewarded by an abundance of cogni-
tions and suggestions; since the Greek period
he was the first to investigate the secrets of nature, relying entirely on his observation and his
own judgment.   But when he learned to de-
preciate authority and to reject the imitation
of the "ancients" and constantly pointed to the
study of nature as the source of all wisdom, he
only repeated in the highest sublimation attainable to man, which had already obtruded
itself on the little boy who surveyed the world
with wonder.   To retranslate the scientific ab-
stractions into concrete individual experiences,
we would say that the "ancients" and authority
only corresponded to the father, and nature
again became the tender mother who nourished
him.   While in most human beings to-day, as
in primitive times, the need for a support of
some authority is so imperative that their world
becomes shaky when their authority is men-
aced, Leonardo alone was able to exist without
such support; but that would not have been

⁶ Solmi, Conf. fior, p. 13.

possible had he not been deprived of his father in the first years of his life. The boldness and independence of his later scientific investigation presupposes that his infantile sexual investigation was not inhibited by his father, and this same spirit of scientific independence was continued by his withdrawing from sex.

If any one like Leonardo escapes in his childhood his father's intimidation and later throws off the shackles of authority in his scientific investigation, it would be in gross contradiction to our expectation if we found that this same man remained a believer and unable to withdraw from dogmatic religion. Psychoanalysis has taught us the intimate connection between the father complex and belief in God, and daily demonstrates to us how youthful persons lose their religious belief as soon as the authority of the father breaks down. In the parental complex we thus recognize the roots of religious need; the almighty, just God, and kindly nature appear to us as grand sublimations of father and mother, or rather as revivals and restorations of the infantile conceptions of both parents. Religiousness is biologically traced to the long period of helplessness and need of help of the little child. When the child grows up and realizes his loneliness and weakness in the presence of the great forces of life, he perceives his condition as in childhood and seeks to disavow his despair through a regressive revival of the protecting forces of childhood.

It does not seem that Leonardo's life disproves this conception of religious belief. Accusations charging him with irreligiousness, which in those times was equivalent to renouncing Christianity, were brought against him already in his lifetime, and were clearly described in the first biography given by Vasari.[7] In the second edition of his Vite (1568) Vasari left out this observation. In view of the extraordinary sensitiveness of his age in matters of religion it is perfectly comprehensible to us why Leonardo refrained from directly expressing his position to Christianity in his notes. As investigator he did not permit himself to be misled by the account of the creation of the holy scriptures; for instance,

[7] Müntz, 1. c., La Religion de Leonardo, p. 292, etc.

he disputed the possibility of a universal flood, and in geology he was as unscrupulous in calculating with hundred thousands of years as modern investigators.

Among his "prophecies" one finds some things that would perforce offend the sensitive feelings of a religious Christian, e.g. Praying to the images of Saints, reads as follows:[8]

"People talk to people who perceive nothing, who have open eyes and see nothing; they shall talk to them and receive no answer; they shall adore those who have ears and hear nothing; they shall burn lamps for those who do not see."

Or: Concerning mourning on Good Friday (p. 297):

"In all parts of Europe great peoples will bewail the death of one man who died in the Orient."

It was asserted of Leonardo's art that he took away the last remnant of religious attachment from the holy figures and put them into human form in order to depict in them great

[8] Herzfeld, p. 292.

and beautiful human feelings.   Muther praises him for having overcome the feeling of decadence, and for having returned to man the right of sensuality and pleasurable enjoyment.   The notices which show Leonardo absorbed in fathoming the great riddles of nature do not lack any expressions of admiration for the creator, the last cause of all these wonderful secrets, but nothing indicates that he wished to hold any personal relation to this divine force.   The sentences which contain the deep wisdom of his last years breathe the resignation of the man who subjects himself to the laws of nature and expects no alleviation from the kindness or grace of God.   There is hardly any doubt that Leonardo had vanquished dogmatic as well as personal religion, and through his work of investigation he had withdrawn far from the world aspect of the religious Christian.

From our views mentioned before in the development of the infantile psychic life, it becomes clear that also Leonardo's first investigations in childhood occupied themselves with the problems of sexuality.   But he himself betrays it to us through a transparent veil, in that he connects his impulse to investigate with the vulture phantasy, and in emphasizing the problem of the flight of the bird as one whose elaboration devolved upon him through special concatenations of fate. A very obscure as well as a prophetically sounding passage in his notes dealing with the flight of the bird demonstrates in the nicest way with how much affective interest he clung to the wish that he himself should be able to imitate the art of flying: "The human bird shall take his first flight, filling the world with amazement, all writings with his fame, and bringing eternal glory to the nest whence he sprang." He probably hoped that he himself would sometimes be able to fly, and we know from the wish fulfilling dreams of people what bliss one expects from the fulfillment of this hope.

But why do so many people dream that they are able to fly? Psychoanalysis answers this question by stating that to fly or to be a bird in the dream is only a concealment of another wish, to the recognition of which one can reach by more than one linguistic or objective bridge.

When the inquisitive child is told that a big bird like the stork brings the little children, when the ancients have formed the phallus winged, when the popular designation of the sexual activity of man is expressed in German by the word "to bird" (vögeln), when the male member is directly called *l'uccello* (bird) by the Italians, all these facts are only small fragments from a large collection which teaches us that the wish to be able to fly signifies in the dream nothing more or less than the longing for the ability of sexual accomplishment. This is an early infantile wish. When the grown-up recalls his childhood it appears to him as a happy time in which one is happy for the moment and looks to the future without any wishes, it is for this reason that he envies children. But if children themselves could inform us about it they would probably give different reports. It seems that childhood is not that blissful Idyl into which we later distort it, that on the contrary children are lashed through the years of childhood by the wish to become big, and to imitate the grown ups. This wish instigates all their playing. If in the course of their sexual investigation children feel that the grown up knows something wonderful in the mysterious and yet so important realm, what they are prohibited from knowing or doing, they are seized with a violent wish to know it, and dream of it in the form of flying, or prepare this disguise of the wish for their later flying dreams. Thus aviation, which has attained its aim in our times, has also its infantile erotic roots.

By admitting that he entertained a special personal relation to the problem of flying since his childhood, Leonardo bears out what we must assume from our investigation of children of our times, namely, that his childhood investigation was directed to sexual matters. At least this one problem escaped the repression which has later estranged him from sexuality. From childhood until the age of perfect intellectual maturity this subject, slightly varied, continued to hold his interest, and it is quite possible that he was as little successful in his cherished art in the primary sexual sense as in his desires for mechanical matters, that both wishes were denied to him.

As a matter of fact the great Leonardo remained infantile in some ways throughout his whole life; it is said that all great men retain something of the infantile. As a grown up he still continued playing, which sometimes made him appear strange and incomprehensible to his contemporaries. When he constructed the most artistic mechanical toys for court festivities and receptions we are dissatisfied thereby because we dislike to see the master waste his power on such petty stuff. He himself did not seem averse to giving his time to such things. Vasari reports that he did similar things even when not urged to it by request: "There (in Rome) he made a doughy mass out of wax, and when it softened he formed thereof very, delicate animals filled with air; when he blew into them they flew in the air, and when the air was exhausted they fell to the ground. For a peculiar lizard caught by the wine-grower of Belvedere Leonardo made wings from skin pulled off from other lizards, which he filled with mercury so that they moved and trembled when it walked; he then made for it eyes, a beard and horns, tamed it and put it in a lit-

tle box and terrified all his friends with it." [9]
Such playing often served him as an expression
of serious thoughts: "He had often cleaned
the intestines of a sheep so well that one could
hold them in the hollow of the hand; he brought
them into a big room, and attached them to
a blacksmith's bellows which he kept in an ad-
jacent room, he then blew them up until they
filled up the whole room so that everybody
had to crowd into a corner. In this manner
he showed how they gradually became transparent and filled up with air, and as they were
at first limited to very little space and gradually became more and more extended in the
big room, he compared them to a genius." [10]
His fables and riddles evince the same playful
pleasure in harmless concealment and artistic
investment, the riddles were put into the form
of prophecies; almost all are rich in ideas and
to a remarkable degree devoid of wit.

The plays and jumps which Leonardo allowed his phantasy have in some cases quite
misled his biographers who misunderstood this

[9] Vasari, translated by Schorn, 1843.
[10] Ebenda, p. 39.

part of his nature. In Leonardo's Milanese manuscripts one finds, for example, outlines of letters to the "Diodario of Sorio (Syria), viceroy of the holy Sultan of Babylon," in which Leonardo presents himself as an engineer sent to these regions of the Orient in ‧ order to construct some works. In these letters he defends himself against the reproach of laziness, he furnishes geographical descriptions of cities and mountains, and finally discusses a big elementary event which occurred while he was there.[11]

In 1881, J. P. Richter had endeavored to prove from these documents that Leonardo made these traveler's observations when he really was in the service of the Sultan of Egypt, and that while in the Orient he embraced the Mohammedan religion. This sojourn in the Orient should have taken place in the time of 1483, that is, before he removed to the court of the Duke of Milan. However, it was not difficult for other authors to recognize the il-

[11] Concerning these letters and the combinations connected with them see Müntz, l. c., p. 82; for the wording of the same and for the notices connected with them see Herzfeld, l. c., p. 223.

lustrations of this supposed journey to the Orient as what they really were, namely, phantastic productions of the youthful artist which he created for his own amusement, and in which he probably brought to expression his wishes to see the world and experience adventures.

A phantastic formation is probably also the "Academia Vinciana," the acceptance of which is due to the existence of five or six most clever and intricate emblems with the inscription of the Academy. Vasari mentions these drawings but not the Academy.[12] Müntz who placed such ornament on the cover of his big work on Leonardo belongs to the few who believe in the reality of an "Academia Vinciana."

It is probable that this impulse to play disappeared in Leonardo's maturer years, that it became discharged in the investigating activity

[12] Besides, he lost some time in that he even made a drawing of a braided cord in which one could follow the thread from one end to the other, until it formed a perfectly circular figure; a very difficult and beautiful drawing of this kind is engraved on copper, in the center of it one can read the words: "Leonardus Vinci Academia" (p. 8).

which signified the highest development of his personality. But the fact that it continued so long may teach us how slowly one tears himself away from his infantilism after having enjoyed in his childhood supreme erotic happiness which is later unattainable.

VI

IT would be futile to delude ourselves that at present, readers find every pathography unsavory. This attitude is excused with the reproach that from a pathographic elaboration of a great man one never obtains an understanding of his importance and his attainments, that it is therefore useless mischief to study in him things which could just as well be found in the first comer. However, this criticism is so clearly unjust that it can only be grasped when viewed as a pretext and a disguise for something. As a matter of fact pathography does not aim at making comprehensible the attainments of the great man; no one should really be blamed for not doing something which one never promised. The real motives for the opposition are quite different. One finds them when one bears in mind that biographers are fixed on their heroes in quite a peculiar manner.

Frequently they take the hero as the object of study because, for reasons of their personal emotional life, they bear him a special affection from the very outset. They then devote themselves to a work of idealization which strives to enroll the great men among their infantile models, and to revive through him, as it were, the infantile conception of the father. For the sake of this wish they wipe out the individual features in his physiognomy, they rub out the traces of his life's struggle with inner and outer resistances, and do not tolerate in him anything of human weakness or imperfection; they then give us a cold, strange, ideal form instead of the man to whom we could feel distantly related. It is to be regretted that they do this, for they thereby sacrifice the truth to an illusion, and for the sake of their infantile phantasies they let slip the opportunity to penetrate into the most attractive secrets of human nature.[1]

Leonardo himself, judging from his love for the truth and his inquisitiveness, would have

[1] This criticism holds quite generally and is not aimed at Leonardo's biographers in particular.

interposed no objections to the effort of dis-
covering the determinations of his psychic and
intellectual development from the trivial peculiarities and riddles of his nature. We respect him by learning from him. It does no
injury to his greatness to study the sacrifices
which his development from the child must
have entailed, and to the compile factors which
have stamped on his person the tragic feature
of failure.

Let us expressly emphasize that we have
never considered Leonardo as a neurotic or as
a "nervous person" in the sense of this awk-
ward term. Whoever takes it amiss that we
should even dare apply to him viewpoints
gained from pathology, still clings to preju-
dices which we have at present justly given up.
We no longer believe that health and disease,
normal and nervous, are sharply distinguished
from each other, and that neurotic traits must
be judged as proof of general inferiority. We
know to-day that neurotic symptoms are substitutive formations for certain repressive acts
which have to be brought about in the course
of our development from the child to the cul-

tural man, that we all produce such substitutive formations, and that only the amount, intensity, and distribution of these substitutive formations justify the practical conception of illness and the conclusion of constitutional inferiority. Following the slight signs in Leonardo's personality we would place him near that neurotic type which we designate as the "compulsive type," and we would compare his investigation with the "reasoning mania" of neurotics, and his inhibitions with the so-called "abulias" of the latter.

The object of our work was to explain the inhibitions in Leonardo's sexual life and in his artistic activity. For this purpose we shall now sum up what we could discover concerning the course of his psychic development.

We were unable to gain any knowledge about his hereditary factors, on the other hand we recognize that the accidental circumstances of his childhood produced a far reaching disturbing effect. His illegitimate birth deprived him of the influence of a father until perhaps his fifth year, and left him to the tender seduction of a mother whose only consolation he was.

Having been kissed by her into sexual prematurity, he surely must have entered into a phase of infantile sexual activity of which only one single manifestation was definitely evinced, namely, the intensity of his infantile sexual investigation. The impulse for looking and inquisitiveness were most strongly stimulated by his impressions from early childhood; the enormous mouth-zone received its accentuation which it had never given up. From his later contrasting behavior, as the exaggerated sympathy for animals, we can conclude that this infantile period did not lack in strong sadistic traits.

An energetic shift of repression put an end to this infantile excess, and established the dispositions which became manifest in the years of puberty. The most striking result of this transformation was a turning away from all gross sensual activities. Leonardo was able to lead a life of abstinence and made the impression of an asexual person. When the floods of pubescent excitement came over the boy they did not make him ill by forcing him to costly and harmful substitutive formations; owing to the early preference for sexual inquisitiveness, the greater part of the sexual needs could be sublimated into a general thirst after knowledge and so elude repression. A much smaller portion of the libido was applied to sexual aims, and represented the stunted sexual life of the grown up. In consequence of the repression of the love for the mother this portion assumed a homosexual attitude and manifested itself as ideal love for boys. The fixation on the mother, as well as the happy reminiscences of his relations with her, was preserved in his unconscious but remained for the time in an inactive state. In this manner the repression, fixation, and sublimation participated in the disposal of the contributions which the sexual impulse furnished to Leonardo's psychic life.

From the obscure age of boyhood Leonardo appears to us as an artist, a painter, and sculptor, thanks to a specific talent which was probably enforced by the early awakening of the impulse for looking in the first years of childhood. We would gladly report in what way the artistic activity depends on the psychic primitive forces were it not that our material is inadequate just here. We content ourselves by emphasizing the fact, concerning which hardly any doubt still exists, that the productions of the artist give outlet also to his sexual desire, and in the case of Leonardo we can refer to the information imparted by Vasari, namely, that heads of laughing women and pretty boys, or representations of his sexual objects, attracted attention among his first artistic attempts. It seems that during his flourishing youth Leonardo at first worked in an uninhibited manner. As he took his father as a model for his outer conduct in life, he passed through a period of manly creative power and artistic productivity in Milan, where favored by fate he found a substitute for his father in the duke Lodovico Moro. But the experience of others was soon confirmed in him, to wit, that the almost complete suppression of the real sexual life does not furnish the most favorable conditions for the activity of the sublimated sexual strivings. The figurativeness of his sexual life asserted itself, his activity and ability to quick decisions began to weaken, the tendency to reflection and

delay was already noticeable as a disturbance
in The Holy Supper, and with the influence of
the technique determined the fate of this magnificent work. Slowly a process developed in
him which can be put parallel only to the re-
gressions of neurotics. His development at
puberty into the artist was outstripped by the
early infantile determinant of the investigator,
the second sublimation of his erotic impulses
turned back to the primitive one which was prepared at the first repression. He became an
investigator, first in service of his art, later
independently and away from his art. With
the loss of his patron, the substitute for his father, and with the increasing difficulties in his
life, the regressive displacement extended in
dimension. He became *"impacientissimo al
pennello"* (most impatient with the brush) as
reported by a correspondent of the countess
Isabella d'Este who desired to possess at any
cost a painting from his hand.[2] His infantile
past had obtained control over him. The investigation, however, which now took the place
of his artistic production, seems to have born

[2] Seidlitz II, p. 271.

certain traits which betrayed the activity of unconscious impulses; this was seen in his insatiability, his regardless obstinacy, and in his lack of ability to adjust himself to actual conditions.

At the summit of his life, in the age of the first fifties, at a time when the sex characteristics of the woman have already undergone a regressive change, and when the libido in the man not infrequently ventures into an energetic advance, a new transformation came over him. Still deeper strata of his psychic content became active again, but this further regression was of benefit to his art which was in a state of deterioration. He met the woman who awakened in him the memory of the happy and sensuously enraptured smile of his mother, and under the influence of this awakening he acquired back the stimulus which guided him in the beginning of his artistic efforts when he formed the smiling woman. He painted Monna Lisa, Saint Anne, and a number of mystic pictures which were characterized by the enigmatic smile. With the help of his oldest erotic feelings he triumphed in conquering once more the inhibition in his art. This last development faded away in the obscurity of the approaching old age. But before this his intellect rose to the highest capacity of a view of life, which was far in advance of his time.

In the preceding chapters I have shown what justification one may have for such representation of Leonardo's course of development, for this manner of arranging his life and explaining his wavering between art and science. If after accomplishing these things I should provoke the criticism from even friends and adepts of psychoanalysis, that I have only written a psychoanalytic romance, I should answer that I certainly did not overestimate the reliability of these results. Like others I succumbed to the attraction emanating from this great and mysterious man, in whose being one seems to feel powerful propelling passions, which after all can only evince themselves so remarkably subdued.

But whatever may be the truth about Leonardo's life we cannot relinquish our effort to investigate it psychoanalytically before we have finished another task. In general we must

mark out the limits which are set up for the
working capacity of psychoanalysis in biography so that every omitted explanation should
not be held up to us as a failure. Psychoanalytic investigation has at its disposal the
data of the history of the person's life, which
on the one hand consists of accidental events
and environmental influences, and on the other
hand of the reported reactions of the individual. Based on the knowledge of psychic mechanisms it now seeks to investigate dynamically
the character of the individual from his reactions, and to lay bare his earliest psychic motive
forces as well as their later transformations
and developments. If this succeeds then the
reaction of the personality is explained through
the coöperation of constitutional and accidental
factors or through inner and outer forces. If
such an undertaking, as perhaps in the case of
Leonardo, does not yield definite results then
the blame for it is not to be laid to the faulty
or inadequate psychoanalytic method, but to
the vague and fragmentary material left by
tradition about this person. It is, therefore,
only the author who forced psychoanalysis to

furnish an expert opinion on such insufficient material, who is to be held responsible for the failure.

However, even if one had at his disposal a very rich historical material and could manage the psychic mechanism with the greatest certainty, a psychoanalytic investigation could not possibly furnish the definite view, if it concerns two important questions, that the individual could turn out only so and not differently. Concerning Leonardo we had to represent the view that the accident of his illegitimate birth and the pampering of his mother exerted the most decisive influence on his character formation and his later fate, through the fact that the sexual repression following this infantile phase caused him to sublimate his libido into a thirst after knowledge, and thus determined his sexual inactivity for his entire later life. The repression, however, which followed the first erotic gratification of childhood did not have to take place, in another individual it would perhaps not have taken place or it would have turned out not nearly as profuse. We must recognize here a degree of freedom which can no longer be solved psychoanalytically. One is as little justified in representing the issue of this shift of repression as the only possible issue. It is quite probable that another person would not have succeeded in withdrawing the main part of his libido from the repression through sublimation into a desire for knowledge; under the same influences as Leonardo another person might have sustained a permanent injury to his intellectual work or an uncontrollable disposition to compulsion neurosis. The two characteristics of Leonardo which remained unexplained through psychoanalytic effort are first, his particular tendency to repress his impulses, and second, his extraordinary ability to sublimate the primitive impulses.

The impulses and their transformations are the last things that psychoanalysis can discern. Henceforth it leaves the place to biological investigation. The tendency to repression, as well as the ability to sublimate, must be traced back to the organic bases of the character, upon which alone the psychic structure springs up. As artistic talent and productive ability are

intimately connected with sublimation we have
to admit that also the nature of artistic attain-
ment is psychoanalytically inaccessible to us.
Biological investigation of our time endeavors
to explain the chief traits of the organic constitution of a person through the fusion of male
and female predispositions in the material
sense; Leonardo's physical beauty as well as
his left-handedness furnish here some support.
However, we do not wish to leave the ground
of pure psychologic investigation. Our aim
remains to demonstrate the connection between
outer experiences and reactions of the person
over the path of the activity of the impulses.
Even if psychoanalysis does not explain to us
the fact of Leonardo's artistic accomplishment,
it still gives us an understanding of the expressions and limitations of the same. It does
seem as if only a man with Leonardo's childhood experiences could have painted Monna
Lisa and Saint Anne, and could have supplied
his works with that sad fate and so obtain un-
heard of fame as a natural historian; it seems
as if the key to all his attainments and failures

was hidden in the childhood phantasy of the
vulture.

But may one not take offense at the results
of an investigation which concede to the accidents of the parental constellation so decisive
an influence on the fate of a person, which, for
example, subordinates Leonardo's fate to his
illegitimate birth and to the sterility of his first
step-mother Donna Albiera? I believe that
one has no right to feel so; if one considers
accident as unworthy of determining our fate,
it is only a relapse to the pious aspect of life,
the overcoming of which Leonardo himself
prepared when he put down in writing that the
sun does not move. We are naturally grieved
over the fact that a just God and a kindly provi-
dence do not guard us better against such influences in our most defenseless age. We
thereby gladly forget that as a matter of fact
everything in our life is accident from our very
origin through the meeting of spermatozoa and
ovum, accident, which nevertheless participates
in the lawfulness and fatalities of nature, and
lacks only the connection to our wishes and

illusions. The division of life's determinants into the "fatalities" of our constitution and the "accidents" of our childhood may still be indefinite in individual cases, but taken altogether one can no longer entertain any doubt about the importance of precisely our first years of childhood. We all still show too little respect for nature, which in Leonardo's deep words recalling Hamlet's speech *"is full of infinite reasons which never appeared in experience."* [8] Every one of us human beings corresponds to one of the infinite experiments in which these "reasons of nature" force themselves into experience.

[8] La natura è piena d'infinite ragionè che non furono mai in' isperienza, M. Herzfeld, 1. c. p. 11.

THE END

.

.

www.ingramcontent.com/pod-product-compliance
Lightning Source LLC
Chambersburg PA
CBHW051438270326
41931CB00019B/3466